Someone Must Survive To Tell The World

Reminiscences

by

Tosia Szechter Schneider

Tosia Schneider

To Shemie with best wishes

Atlanta 2007 Montreal

PODZIĘKOWANIA

Wyrażamy wdzięczność
Polskiej Fundacji Społeczno-Kulturalnej
za wsparcie finansowe
naszego projektu wydawniczego.

Someone Must Survive To Tell The World
Tosia Szechter Schneider

Cover etching "Hands" by Beata Wehr

Komitet redakcyjny:
Andrea Axt, Ilona Gruda, Alina Kopeć, Agata Kozanecka

ISBN 978-0-9783014-1-5

Polish-Jewish Heritage Foundation of Canada

PRZEDMOWA

Oto dwunasty opublikowany tom naszej kolekcji
Aby nie zapomnieć - Pour ne pas oublier - Let us not forget

Pragniemy przede wszystkim podziękować autorce za zgodę na opublikowanie Jej wspomnień okupacyjnych oraz za przyjazną współpracę w przygotowaniu publikacji.

Żyje jeszcze wiele rozsianych po całym świecie osób, które przeżyły w Polsce nieludzki okres okupacji niemieckiej podczas drugiej wojny światowej. Historia każdej z nich składa się z szeregu niespodziewanych wydarzeń, tragicznych lub zbawiennych spotkań, trudnych do powzięcia decyzji i cudownych ocaleń. Ludzie ci nie są już młodzi i jeśli do tej pory nie opublikowali swoich wspomnień z tamtego okresu, istnieje możliwość, że nigdy już tego nie zrobią. A przecież świadectwa te są niezwykle ważne z punktu widzenia historycznego, psychologicznego, czy po prostu ludzkiego. Chcemy i powinniśmy wiedzieć jakie to były czasy i jakimi okazywali się ludzie w dramatycznych lub wręcz tragicznych okolicznościach totalnego zagrożenia. Czego możemy się spodziewać w skrajnych sytuacjach po obcych, po naszych bliskich, po nas samych. Im więcej zgromadzimy świadectw tamtych czasów, tym nasza wiedza o świecie będzie bogatsza, nasze zrozumienie zjawisk - głębsze. Nie należy dopuścić do tego, aby te świadectwa zniknęły wraz ze świadkami. Są one ponadto pomnikiem wystawionym tym, którym nie udało się przeżyć tych tragicznych czasów. Ważnym jest, aby pamięć o nich nie zaginęła.

Nasza organizacja (Polish-Jewish Heritage Foundation) stawia sobie za cel wynajdywanie napisanych już wspomnień, aby je opublikować i przekazać do odpowiednich bibliotek. Pragniemy również skłonić tych, którzy noszą się z zamiarem napisania, aby nie zwlekali z przekazaniem potomności swojego świadectwa.

Publikujemy te wspomnienia w języku, w którym zostały napisane, z pełnym zaufaniem co do ich autentyczności.

INTRODUCTION

You are holding the twelfth publication in our series,
Aby nie zapomnieć - Pour ne pas oublier - Let us not forget

We would like to express our thanks to the author for agreeing to publish her wartime recollections and for friendly cooperation during the process.

A number of people who survived the German Occupation of Poland during W.W.II are still alive and scattered around the world. The personal history of every one of those individuals is woven into a series of momentous events: tragic or fortunate encounters, fateful life decisions, and miraculous deliverances. The people in question are not young anymore and since they have not published their memoirs by now, it is doubtful that they will ever do so. There is, however, no question that these testimonies are enormously important historical records. They tell us much about those perilous times; about how people behaved in dramatic, dangerous, and often tragic circumstances. They tell us what we might expect from strangers, from those close to us, and from ourselves. The more testimonies we have from those times, the broader will be our knowledge of the world around us and the more profound our understanding of it. We must not allow the facts to fade away into oblivion as the witnesses pass on. We must ensure, too, that those who did not survive are never forgotten.

The aim of the Polish-Jewish Heritage Foundation is to seek out and publish the testimonies of survivors in order to distribute them into libraries. We will encourage those who are inclined to write, but have not gotten around to doing so, not to delay recording their experiences for the benefit of future generations. We will publish all testimonies in the language in which they were written with all confidence to their authenticity.

INTRODUCTION

Voilà le douzième volume de notre collection
Aby nie zapomnieć - Pour ne pas oublier - Let us not forget

Nous voulons tout d'abord remercier l'auteure d'avoir accepté la publication de ses mémoires de guerre ainsi que pour sa collaboration amicale au cours de la publication.

Éparpillés tout autour du monde, vivent encore des gens qui ont survécu en Pologne les temps inhumains de l'occupation allemande pendant la deuxième guerre mondiale. L'histoire de chacun d'eux est composée d'un grand nombre d'événements inattendus, de rencontres tragiques ou salutaires, de décisions difficiles à prendre, de sauvetages miraculeux. Ces gens ne sont plus jeunes et s'ils n'ont pas encore écrit et publié leur mémoires, il est probable qu'ils ne le fassent jamais. Et pourtant, ces témoignages sont extrêmement importants du point de vu historique, psychologique et, tout simplement humain. Nous voulons et nous devons savoir comment les gens se comportaient dans des circonstances dangereuses, dramatiques, souvent tragiques. À quoi nous pouvons nous attendre de la part des étrangers, des nos proches, des nous mêmes.

Plus il y aura de témoignages des cette époque, plus notre connaissance du monde sera riche, notre compréhension des événements - profonde. Il ne faut pas permettre que ces témoignages disparaissent avec les témoins. Nous devrons aussi nous assurer que ceux qui n'ont pas réussi à survivre ne soient pas oubliés.

La Fondation de l'héritage polono-juif se propose de retracer des mémoires du temps de guerre, que les gens ont écrits sans les publier, de les publier et les distribuer dans les bibliothèques. Nous voulons aussi encourager ceux qui n'ont pas osé mettre sur papier leurs témoignages de le faire au profit de la postérité.

Nous publions ces mémoires dans la langue dans laquelle ils ont été écrits avec toute confiance en leur authenticité.

Acknowledgements

I would like to take this opportunity to thank my husband of 57 years, who listened to my stories, and comforted me when nightmares disturbed my sleep. He made the difficult adjustment to a new life and a new country easier for me. He is my best friend and my mentor.

I am deeply grateful to Professor Mel Konner, who through the years encouraged me to write a memoir.

I would also like to thank my friends at the Breman Jewish Museum in Atlanta, who urged me to write this memoir, to bear witness.

MEMORIAM TO MY FAMILY WHO DIED IN THE SHOAH

Jacob Szechter, father

Genia Meltzer Szechter, mother

Julek Szechter, brother

Zirl Meltzer, grandmother

May their memory be blessed forever.

TABLE OF CONTENTS

Foreword

For many years I have known Tosia Szechter Schneider as an elegant, cultivated, charming woman, a mother and grandmother who takes pride in her family, in her long career as a teacher, in her role as the loving wife of a distinguished nuclear engineer, and in her six decades as an American. Only a slight, almost musical accent hints at the life she lived until age eighteen, before coming to America; that, and a far-off look that comes over her at times, along with a polite distaste for most things German.

I knew she had a story – or rather, a thousand stories – connected with her lost life in a beautiful East European village where she had spent an idyllic childhood. I knew that this sweet, good life and all the structures and institutions and people that made it so were smashed and ground into dust or burned into smoky air by German "warriors" obsessed with the murder of Jews. And I knew – from the evidence of her present life and the infectious smile that so often lit up her face – that the story had, in some ways, against all probability, a very happy ending.

I also knew that she was planning to write about her life in that apocalyptic time, and that those far-off looks probably meant that her peace – at a Sabbath dinner in her home, at a beloved son's wedding, or at a pleasant French restaurant in Atlanta – was being invaded by dreadful memories. I certainly hoped that she would set them down, that she would grapple with the challenge of her beloved mother – dying because she had given too much of her own food to her children – "Someone must survive to tell the world".

I was born in 1946 to American parents who told me my conception had been postponed until the closing of the gas chambers. I learned to talk during the Nuremberg trials, when the air, even in faraway Brooklyn, was dense with dreadful revelations. My Orthodox synagogue was full of new Americans who alluded, in Yiddish and other, to-me-strange, tongues, to what I dimly understood was their season in Hell. Their stories seemed fantastic and hard to believe, and as the years passed they fell silent.

But I became obsessed with what, for excellent reasons, they only wanted to forget. I am not a Holocaust historian, but I have read a good deal of the literature on this greatest lapse in the moral advance of our species. I have seen most of the films, taught and written about it, talked about it to anyone who would listen, and listened to anyone with real knowledge willing to talk to me. For someone who started life as a naïve and protected American, I am quite familiar with the facts, and with just about every way that survivors and historians have found to describe them.

Yet Tosia Schneider's memoir has been a revelation to me, and I have tried to understand why. The marvelous diaries of Anne Frank, Hannah Senesh, and Etty Hillesum are also touching and personal. But they are in the moment, and none of these young women lived to reflect back on the lives so starkly cut short; their pens fell from their hands before they could grasp the extent of the crimes against their people. Primo Levi and Paul Celan turned their nightmares and their pain into exquisite literature, but each of these men succumbed to his interminable despair, ending by his own hand the life Hitler's minions had failed to extinguish.

Tosia Schneider's memoir combines simplicity, immediacy, emotional depth, reflection, and, above all perhaps, a triumph of the spirit that makes it something different and wonderful. There is no detachment here, and no lack of awareness of the magnitude of the horror. There is anger, to be sure, and a perfectly healthy desire for revenge. But most of all there is love – this book is a tender, loving account of a family, a wide web of grandparents, uncles, aunts, cousins, and friends, a story of an attachment to a place, a home, a panorama of memories. And every person, every affection, every event, small or large, comes vividly alive.

Like her life today, her childhood was filled with happiness, and even the difficulties of a relatively poor family in pre-war Eastern Europe give rise to sweet memories. This part of the memoir reads almost like an idyll. A little girl finds her family's apartment building "a marvelous place to explore", and delights in the tiny springs a watchmaker gives her to play with. The bread lady's basket brims over with rich aromas and the girl is allowed her favorite pastry, an almond bear-claw. She glows with pride when given her own little wine-cup at Passover. She and her brother weed and water the family garden, which yields all manner of fruits and vegetable for their table. She becomes Queen of the Snowflakes in a Chanukah pageant. Despite the socks and gloves her grandmother lovingly knits for her, she gets a little frostbite because she loves to play in the snow. She and her friends also play at war – they are still in the long shadow of World War I – but it's only a game.

There are some bad signs. Polish children sometimes yell anti-Semitic epithets. A new municipal swimming pool bars Jews, and she and her friends stroll by it longingly. Her father must wash "Out with the Jews!" from the wall of their home. Quotas are imposed on Jewish school and college attendance. New laws prohibit Jewish ritual slaughter, very hard on Orthodox Jews. This is mere home-grown Polish anti-Semitism, years before the German invasion, but it is intensifying. The Poles and the Germans are enemies, but they agree about the Jews.

Still, the invasion changes everything. Events we are all now familiar with, even numb to, stab the heart again because of Schneider's way of personalizing them as particular instances of love and loss. The opening bombing raid of the war kills a Jewish child, the first of thousands in Horodenka alone; his father carries him to the cemetery and buries him, refusing all help. When Jews must don the Star of David, young women embroider exquisite ones for the young men they love, a silent discourse of romance and defiance. A friend of the family stumbles sobbing into their hiding place, having just recognized in a pile of seized clothing the dress his wife had worn when she was taken away, and they do their best to comfort him.

These are acts of resistance, of spiritual victory, of utter, decisive refusal to be dehumanized. But they are only the first salvos in the unrelenting war against the Jews. Brutality deepens, choices narrow. Tosia's brother, a slave laborer, must pave the German commandant's courtyard with gravestones from the Jewish cemetery. German strictures promote the spread of typhus while withholding all medicines and prohibiting Jewish doctors from helping. When they are forced into a savagely cramped and disease-ridden ghetto, Tosia must leave her kitten behind; there will be no food for it. On pain of death they deliver all they own of value to the Germans, except for her grandmother's beloved Sabbath candlesticks, which they help her bury in the garden. Tosia's blond hair and "Aryan" beauty attract German men who offer help but who are interested in something quite different. The same good looks lead to several real chances for escape; repeatedly, she rejects them to stand by what is left of her family.

These are the personal touches by which Tosia Schneider makes well-known horrors regain their meaning and, after all the incomprehensible statistics we have seen again and again, reawakens our shock and sympathy. This is no generic litany of crimes, but instead the story of one girl, the brave young woman she became, and her inspiring resilience and courage. It is a story of unimaginable tragedy and yet of transcendent human dignity and final personal triumph.

Yes, it is a horror story, and a true one, in which the monsters are neither giant goblins nor ravenous space aliens but something much worse: these monsters are dressed in German uniforms. They are real. But the horror story is bracketed by an account of a beautiful childhood, a celebration of love and tenderness and loss, a living memorial to gifted and generous human beings who were destined to be murdered for one reason only; and by the story of a survivor who not only lived to tell the world, but who created a loving family of her own, a family that is a mirror image of the love and gifts and decency of the family she lost.

This new family, which Tosia Szechter Schneider created out of her own body and heart and soul, is the final decisive answer to the vicious but failed attempt to destroy her and her people, root and branch. True, she still has occasional nightmares; how could she not? Yet through sheer courage and will, she became a new root for a new large branch of her own family tree – the re-founder of her family – and a new branch of the tree of the Jewish people. And through this horrifying yet touching and beautiful book, she creates countless emotional links between her lost world and each of us, her readers. This is her final victory. May her readers and her offspring be, like Abraham's, as numerous as the stars.

Melvin Konner

Melvin Konner, M.D., Ph.D., is Samuel Candler Dobbs Professor in the Department of Anthropology and the Jewish Studies Program at Emory University. He is the author of *Unsettled: An Anthropology of the Jews* and the forthcoming *The Jewish Body*, among other works.

Childhood

When I think of Zaleszczyki, what comes to mind first is the beautiful horse-chestnut tree in front of our window. It was so lovely in full bloom when it looked like big white candles on a giant Christmas tree. The chestnuts that we so eagerly collected provided for us children many happy hours of play. The stains on our hands from cracking the chestnuts' spiky green outer shells were difficult to wash away and our stained clothes were a great annoyance to our maid.

My birthplace Zaleszczyki is in the part of Galicia, which was Polish before World War II and is now part of the Ukraine. I spent many hours explaining to people that this was once part of the Austro-Hungarian Empire, as well as Russia. The area suffered numerous invasions and changes of regimes. Zaleszczyki was a small resort town on the Dniester River, which formed the border between Poland and Romania.

My father's family, the Szechters (sometimes the spelling was Schechter) lived in Torsk, a small village near Zaleszczyki.

We lived in an apartment house , which belonged to my uncle, Dr. Rosenbaum. There was a large inner courtyard with flowerbeds in the center and facing the street were a few offices and stores. It was a marvelous world to explore. In one of the front offices was a watchmaker's place. What fun it was to watch him doing his work with that long funny instrument on his eye. He always gave us old springs to play with. Next door was a telegraph office where we listened to the mysterious clicking of the telegraph. We usually came home with a bunch of telegraph paper rolls.

One of our playmates was Jan "pokutnik" (Jan the Penitent). Jan lived in our barn and on most days he could be found sitting in front of the nearby Catholic Church, begging for alms. He had shoulder length shaggy gray hair, wore rags and walked barefoot most of the time. He was a very simple minded man who loved children and often played with us. No one ever knew or remembered the reason for his penance. It was told that he had a well-to-do brother in America who sent him clothes and money, but he preferred to live as he did. One day my brother and I got small cork guns and aimed them at Janek. He fell on the floor and pretended to be dead. It was great fun, till my mother walked into the kitchen, and when she saw Jan stretched out on the floor, she almost fainted. We did not know why she got so frightened since Jan was such a good sport.

Almost every morning we waited with anticipation for the "bread" lady to come by. She was a poor Jewish woman who walked from house to house selling sweet rolls and breads. She carried a big basket filled with the most delicious breads and rolls and covered with a clean white towel. What sweet aromas rose from that basket! It took my brother and me quite a while to make our final selections; after a lot of deliberation, I usually picked an almond covered bear claw pastry, my favorite even today.

On the main street of our town, was an ice cream parlor with a white picket fence around it. I loved to sit at the little round marble tables and savor my favorite ice cream. One day, when my father took me for a walk and an ice cream treat, he said that he wanted to tell me something important. He told me that I had a twin brother, whose name was Janek and that he had lived only six weeks. Father said that one day he would take me to the cemetery and show me his grave. I don't think I understood very well what death meant but his expression was so sad and I also felt very sad.

My father Jacob Szechter worked at that time, I believe,

at the estate of Count Lubomirski. I must have been three or four years old when my father took me along with him to visit the estate. We rode in a handsome horse-drawn carriage and on the way my father instructed me how to greet our hosts: I was to kiss their hands and curtsy. When the time came, I did a respectable curtsy but I refused to kiss their hands, very much to my poor father's embarrassment. I still think it was a silly custom. After showing me around the magnificent estate, with its horses, cattle, and hunting dogs, I was put to bed in one of the rooms. The walls of the room were studded with all kinds of stuffed animal heads. The big boar's head was especially frightening. To my father's great dismay, I refused to sleep there and did not stop crying until he promised to take me home. Not a glorious ending, to be sure, but what a relief to be home again.

My brother Julek, two years older than I, was always my close companion, as we explored the world around us. He was a quiet, serious boy, quite the opposite of his tomboy sister. The summers were an exciting time in Zaleszczyki, with many tourists arriving from far-away places. Lovely little boutiques lined the main street of the town and mannequins in swimsuits that always fascinated me stood on the sidewalks. In the summer, my mother used to take us swimming to the Dniester River almost daily. There were two beaches on the river: the "Sunny Beach", which we visited in the morning and the "Shady Beach" for the afternoons. Or was it the other way around? I don't quite remember. But what I do remember is the fun we had frolicking in the river and playing with friends. At the height of the season, the military band of the border guards played on the bandstand while grown-ups strolled and children played. Everyone admired the handsome Romanian officers who sometimes crossed the bridge to participate in some of the festivities.

Every afternoon, during the summer months, in all the coffeehouses that lined the main street, the "fife", as we used to call it, was in full swing. At five o'clock the bands played dance music and the young people danced and sipped cool beverages. This was an opportunity for the locals to meet people from far away places, and of course, romances flourished.

At the end of the summer season, a very festive celebration took place, the "winobranie" (grape harvest). At these festivities, beautifully decorated baskets of grapes were formally presented to the mayor. I believe that Zaleszczyki was the only place in Poland where grapes grew and we took great pride in that fact. Young boys and girls dressed in traditional Polish costumes with flower wreaths on their heads carried the baskets of newly picked grapes through town. Of course, there was music and dancing. It was a much awaited and colorful celebration.

My paternal grandmother and my father's sister's family, the Rosenbaums, lived in Zaleszczyki. My uncle Rosenbaum was a respected doctor who helped bring me into the world. His hobby was growing all kinds of fruit trees, especially apricots, plums, and grapes. He used to experiment and develop new varieties of fruits and was very proud of his achievements. The garden was next door to our house, surrounded by a high wall and a securely locked gate.

My two cousins, Lusia and Julia, were a few years older than I. They were for me a source of much wonder and sophistication. We visited and played together quite often. The language spoken in their house was German, but we spoke Polish at home; I guess their parents never reconciled themselves to the fact that they were no longer citizens of the great Austro-Hungarian Empire and they looked up to Germany and German culture with great admiration. Later, during the war, the knowledge of German became an important factor in saving one of my cousin's life.

The Rosenbaum family lived in a large house in the center of town. The inner courtyard was entered through a heavy wooden gate that was securely locked for the night. On the upper floor was my uncle's surgery, as well as the family's living quarters. On the same floor also lived my grandmother and the family of my uncle's sister, the Zenezibs. On the ground floor facing the street were several stores. The balcony facing the street was my favorite place; I liked to sit there and watch the world go by.

Grandmother always welcomed us with hugs and sweets and we enjoyed very much playing in her apartment. She was an orthodox Jewish lady, who wore the traditional wig. I was always intrigued by a glass container, standing on her cabinet, in which she kept a strand of her once beautiful red hair.

My mother's best friend in town was Salcia Pressner and we often played with the Pressner children. I loved to listen to my mother's stories about their lives as young students at a teacher's college. One of the funniest stories was about matchmaking, quite common in those days. Salcia was an attractive young lady from a well-to-do family and many matchmakers called to arrange a "beshau" (a Yiddish word literally meaning "looking over"), a visit by a prospective groom to meet a young lady. She described one hilarious episode when her friend, fed up with all that fuss, refused to meet the young man alone and insisted that my mother be with her in the room. The young man arrived, was totally confused, and did not know which of the two girls was the one the matchmaker had extolled so highly, all this to the great merriment of the two friends.

I always loved to hear stories about my parents' first meeting. One day my father drove by in a handsome carriage and spotted my mother. Apparently, it was love at first sight. He courted her for quite a while and, even though he was about twelve years older, he finally captured her heart. I have a photograph of my mother in a beautiful Gypsy costume; I learned last year from an old family friend that my father had brought that costume for her from Vienna for a Purim ball.

Their wedding took place in the winter and I heard stories about the wedding guests from my mother's hometown of Horodenka driving their sleds over the frozen Dniester River. As was the custom among our people, the wedding lasted for several days.

In the middle of the thirties, my mother's best friend and her family emigrated to France, very much to my mother's distress. Mother began to study French and she corresponded frequently with her friend. Salcia wrote detailed stories about the fabulous City of Light and her yearly visits home were always greatly anticipated and were a source of great joy for my mother.

At the age of five, I started to attend a Jewish kindergarten. I still recall some of the songs we were taught. My teacher was a tall, blond, lovely lady. It was a bit of a shock when I met her in Israel, forty years later, by now a small, gray-haired woman. One day, our class went on an outing near the bridge over the Dniester River. As we settled down for our lunch, we were pelted with rocks by a group of Polish kids, shouting anti-Semitic slurs at us. For me, it was the first, but sadly not the last time, to witness anti-Semitism raise its ugly head in Poland.

I remember the sled rides in the winter and the wonderful taste of hot cocoa afterward. We had a maid, a Ukrainian girl, who told us scary stories about Baba Jaga, the bad witch, who snatches misbehaving children and takes them to her forest hideout.

When I was about four, our family traveled to my mother's hometown of Horodenka for the Passover holidays. I shall never forget the excitement and the joy of meeting my aunts Zlata and Mincia, uncle Jacob, my many cousins and, of course, my grandparents. My grandmother took me to the bakery where the matzos (traditional unleavened bread) were being baked. At long tables women and girls mixed the dough and flattened it into round matzos, which the baker then placed in the hot, wood-burning ovens. The excitement and the speed of the work fascinated me. The finished matzos were collected in large white sheets and carried home. They were stored high on top of a cabinet, not to be touched till Passover eve. My grandfather David assembled all the grandchildren the afternoon before the Seder (the ceremonial meal on the eve of Passover), and gave each grandchild a little glass cup for the Seder. My cup had the Hebrew word "Pesach" (Passover) inscribed on it. I was so proud to have my own Pesach "wine" cup.

As the evening approached, the whole family was gathered around a long festive table. My grandfather wore a white "kittel" (a silken white robe) and he reclined on the cushions in his chair, as was customary. I can still see the glowing happy faces of my parents and the whole family. As the evening progressed, the Haggadah (the story of the exodus) was read, songs were sung and the traditional foods were eaten, but I had fallen asleep long before the evening ended. This was my first and the most memorable Passover.

When I was six years old, we moved to my mother's hometown of Horodenka. It was a typical East European "shtetl" (little town). The main street was lined with mostly Jewish stores. There was a "drogeria" were cosmetics were sold. The store was owned by my mother's good friend, Shancia Wagner. Mother usually stopped to chat with her after we did our errands. I loved to look at the lovely displays of perfumes, powders and other cosmetics. I usually came home with a little mirror or some other treasure. Only two stores down was another cosmetic store. The two storeowners were archenemies. Needless to say, our little town could hardly support two such stores. On that main street were also a very nice bookstore, a fabric store, a shoe store, as well as a grocery store where we shopped. Also there was the only hotel and restaurant in town run by a Jewish family.

Strzelecka Street, where my grandmother lived, was in a middle class Jewish residential neighborhood, but a few commercial enterprises were also located there. At one corner of Strzelecka Street was a soda factory, at the other end of the street a large dairy. Across the soda factory, lived and worked an elderly Jewish rope maker who sported a long white beard. I liked to watch him as he walked back and forth with an apron tied around his waist stuffed with hemp that he fed into the spinning wheel.

Various craftsmen lived in abject poverty on the side streets in the Jewish part of town, close to the large synagogue. There were carpenters, blacksmiths, shoemakers, harness makers, and tanners. I disliked passing by the tanner's place because of the unpleasant odor. One winter though, I went with my mother to choose a "kozuszek", a sheepskin coat. It had beautifully embroidered borders on the sleeves and collar and it was very warm. After the initial odor of new fur wore off, I loved very much wearing it.

In the center of town, close to where we built our new house, was a carriage stand. Many of the coachmen were Jews. Some had fancy carriages to take people to the railroad station or on trips to nearby villages or towns, but some were simple wagons for transporting goods. One could also hire there a porter for carrying heavy loads.

The largest commercial enterprise in our town was a sugar factory that processed sugar beets, an abundant crop in our region, but Jews could rarely get a job there.

My favorite spot in town was a "cukiernia", a combined pastry shop, coffee house and corner candy store. It was owned by the parents of my best friend Genia Reis, and it was located in the lower level of their house. For one penny one could still get some candy in those days. Of course, my friend and I enjoyed special privileges.

The first year after we arrived in Horodenka, we lived at my grandmother's house. I recall my first religious instruction, repeating after my grandmother the morning prayer in Hebrew, and her wonderful smile when I finally got it right. I enjoyed the warm atmosphere of my mother's extended family and I liked my big cousins, Wisia, Bella and Max Rosenbaum who lived nearby, but I was saddened to discover that my youngest cousin Wisia was deafmute. She was a beautiful child, with dark red curls. I felt a deep sorrow for my aunt and uncle. In their efforts to find help for her, they took her to a specialist in Vienna where she was taught sign language.

Grandmother's house stood at the edge of a ravine. At the bottom of the ravine flowed a small brook. I spent many happy hours with my brother, cousins and friends playing near that stream. We liked to hang out at an abandoned little flourmill that was once powered by a large water wheel. The wheel was covered with moss and was very slippery. We liked to set it in motion and the bravest among us, tried to ride on it. Over the ravine was a bridge that led to an outlying suburb, Kotokuwka, populated mostly by Ukrainians.

In that deep ravine near the stream, we staged all kinds of wars and won great battles. In those days, it was taken for granted that the girls were the nurses, while the boys were always the heroes. There were a few earth-covered mounts in the ravine and stories were told that some of the last war's dead soldiers were buried there. I remember a feeling of unease while playing nearby. I am now certain that the boys told us these tales to test our courage.

My father got a job as an accountant in a large flourmill owned by three Jewish families. He worked very hard but did not earn much and we lived very frugally. A year later, my parents bought a parcel of land and built a small house close to the center of town. We went often to the site and inspected the progress of the construction. I could not wait to move in, since our new house was next-door to the girls' elementary school that I attended. (In my town boys and girls attended separate schools.) There were two apartments in the house, each consisting of two rooms and a kitchen. My parents rented one apartment and the rent from this apartment was set aside for Julek's future education. My parents hoped to send him abroad to study, preferably to England, since in Poland a "numerus clausus" had been introduced for the admission of Jewish students. Admission to higher education was becoming more difficult for Jews and a higher education for girls was rather rare. One also had to pay tuition in high school and Hebrew school, which we attended every afternoon. Our Hebrew school was rather progressive. Unlike some of the very religious schools in town, we received not only religious instruction, but also studied Hebrew grammar, literature, as well as history. In the winter, by four o'clock in the afternoon is was already dark. We sat on narrow benches, boys and girls together, in a dimly lit room and, on occasion, we had a hard time keeping awake, especially when one of the subjects we liked least, Hebrew speed reading, was taught.

The other apartment was rented to my mother's friend, Shancia Wagner. Our families spent a lot of time together. Their only son Manek was a year younger than I, and I thought he was cute but a bit spoiled being an only child. We spent many evenings in the summer sitting in the garden or listening to music on their radio. In the late thirties, the news from Germany was very troubling and my mother always worried about her brother Jacob who lived in Leipzig. My uncle was a chemist who had specialized in the dyeing of furs and he reassured the family that his boss, although a Nazi, liked him and had promised to protect him. How naive they all were in those days!

We had a large garden surrounded by a wooden fence. A good part of the fruits and vegetables for our family came from our garden. Each spring, large sections of the garden were planted with corn and potatoes. We grew our own tomatoes, cucumbers, onions, carrots, as well as all kinds of herbs. We had apple, pear, and plum trees and also strawberries. Spring planting was done with hired help but the weeding and watering of the garden were my brother's and my chores. I often got lost in the strawberry patch and did copious sampling while I worked. Artificial fertilizers, pesticides, or other chemicals were never used, so it was perfectly safe to eat the unwashed strawberries.

The Hebrew school was a short distance from our house; classes were held daily from three to five. Many years later, I used to tell my American students in Sunday school, that this was not considered cruel and unusual punishment. We loved our Hebrew school whose principal, Itzchak Berger was a poet and a very kind man. He never passed a child without saying a kind word. I have always wondered how these poorly paid teachers, working in overcrowded dark classrooms were able to instill in us children so much love and respect for our heritage and our faith, which was to be severely tried a few years later.

I started first grade in the Polish public school. Since the school was located next door to our house, I sometimes jumped over the fence to get there. School started at eight o'clock, and we got home at noon. Dinner, our main meal, was served around one o'clock and my father usually came home for dinner. During the summer months, dinner usually consisted of a vegetable soup. My mother often asked me in the morning to pick carrots, sweet peas, parsnip, and beans from our garden and to dig up some of the new potatoes to be served with chicken or beef. The herbs most frequently used were dill and parsley. Buttered new potatoes with dill were my favorite. Dessert was not part of the meal, except on holidays and Shabbat, but fruits were always plentiful. My father read his favorite Polish-Jewish newspaper the "Chwila" (Moment), rested for an hour, and then went back to work. Supper was usually a very light meal, a sandwich or a pasta dish with freshly made noodles. It was a special treat when mother made "pierogy" – pasta dough stuffed with cheese or potatoes and onions.

In the Polish school, we Jewish children never quite felt on an equal footing with the other kids. To be awarded a prize, one had to be three times as good as a Polish child. I socialized mostly with other Jewish children.

It was at that time that Genia Reis and I became inseparable childhood friends. She lived just a few houses away from my grandmother's and we played together almost daily. She loved comic books and dreamed of America where she had an aunt. We were all enamored with Shirley Temple. We wore Shirley Temple rings, played with cut-out dolls of Shirley Temple, and went to see her movies whenever we could get a few pennies together. Genia had a brother, Lusiek, who was my brother's best friend, and a budding violinist (their mother was a very fine violinist). I had a youthful crush on Lusiek but, to my great dismay, he did not even seem to notice that I existed.

We lived very close to the town's public park. I loved to sit at the window and watch young couples stroll by. On nice summer days, especially on Shabbat, most people would wear their best clothes and stroll up and down the city street. Girls in groups, on one side of the road and the boys on the other. They would steal glances at each other, whisper and giggle. In spring, as the lilac bloomed in our garden and bird songs were heard, the world seemed perfect and beautiful and so full of promise…

On many Sundays my father and my brother were busy with their extensive stamp collection. My father, an avid philatelist received letters from far-away places. I was fascinated by the triangular stamps that came from faraway Africa. It was then that I first learned about the U.S.A., that fabulous country across the ocean that later was to become my home. My father's sister lived in New York and her letters were eagerly awaited.

In winter, we went skiing and ice-skating and one year we decided to build our own ice-skating ring. My brother and Lusiek were the engineers and Genia and I were the water carriers. It was all great fun, but pneumonia followed shortly afterward and I had to stay in bed for quite a while. During the first few days, I liked to burrow deep into my warm feather quilt and watch my brother get ready for school, but after a while I was bored. One day, when I saw my mother sitting on my bed with tears in her eyes, I began to wonder how seriously ill I was. In those days, doctors used to make house calls and at one point my doctor prescribed "cupping". An old lady came to the house, unpacked her glass cups, lit a candle, held the lit candle in the cup for a few seconds and then placed it on my back. Needless to say, I did not like the whole procedure, and I made my feelings known. When she removed the cups red circles covered my chest and back. I was recently amused to see in an alternative medicine "Wellness Center" that cupping has made a comeback.

The big excitement of the winter season was the annual Chanukah play staged by our Hebrew school. One year, I was chosen to be the queen of the snowflakes in a winter wonderland scene. My mother sewed for me a long white gown with lots of glittering sequins. A crown was placed on my head with my long blond hair flowing down on my back as I sat on a sled pulled onto the stage by the snowflakes who then all danced around me. All went well for a while until, as was customary, candies started to be thrown onto the stage by the appreciative audience and one landed in my eye. Thus, my first and last public appearance on a stage ended in tears.

As spring approached, preparations began in earnest for the Passover holidays. It was a common sight to see furniture and dishes stacked in the yard while the kitchens were whitewashed and the rooms were painted. As time drew nearer, the holiday dishes were taken down from the attic and the geese were force-fed to make them plump and ready. The house was cleaned from top to bottom. I especially enjoyed helping to polish the living room floor. Paste was applied to our burgundy colored floor, brushes were attached to our feet and then we danced around the room till one could see one's face reflected by the floor. The beating of the runners was less fun, but the house looked so nice and clean when all the chores were done. A few days before the holidays, the kitchen utensils were made "kosher for Pesach". They were placed in large kettles filled with water and then red-hot stones were thrown inside. The steam was rising and the work was speeding up but we kids always got in the way. We usually got new outfits for the holidays.

When the Passover holiday coincided with Good Friday, there was always some apprehension in the community. Some ruffians in town found this to be an opportune time to attack Jews with shouts of "Christ killers".

One summer, my father took me on a trip to visit our family in Zaleszczyki. I was very excited and prepared for the trip for many days. The day of our departure finally arrived and my mother packed sandwiches, hard-boiled eggs, fresh rolls and fruit, all in a neat basket covered with a white napkin. Early in the morning, a horse-drawn carriage arrived to bring us to the railroad station. What an excitement! It was only a journey of 20 or 30 km, but for me it was a great adventure. For a short distance we traveled through Romanian territory where the train cars were sealed, so when I got home I told everyone that I had traveled abroad. All of this for a thirty miles trip.

When I was growing up, children always helped around the house. There were no laborsaving appliances, so fetching wood for the stove, or storing food in the cold cellar (there were no refrigerators) were our chores. I liked to go down into the cellar on hot summer days and feel the cold damp walls. The chilled sour cream and yogurt tasted so good with freshly picked strawberries from our garden. We had pear and apple trees and a wonderful plum tree. In the last few years before the war, my father planted three peach trees. We never tasted their fruits, because in accordance with Jewish law, one is not allowed to eat the fruits till the fourth year. In that fourth year the war broke out and our world was destroyed forever.

The housewives in town started shopping on Thursdays for the Sabbath. Usually one purchased a live chicken that was taken to the "shochet" who performed the ritual slaughter. Sometimes I went with my mother to the "shochet" but I did not like seeing all that blood. Afterwards, the feathers were plucked and the bird was salted to make it "kosher" before cooking.

Friday morning the cleaning began in earnest. The kitchen table was scrubbed with a brush and soap, as was the wooden floor, and clean kitchen runners were spread on the floor. The wonderful smells of freshly baked "Chalah", the traditional braided white loafs of bread, and of cinnamon and raisin loafs filled the house.

Now it was time for the weekly bath. When my father came home, before my hair was washed and combed, the usual discussion began. "Why don't you cut her hair and stop this yammering when you try to comb out her tangled hair?" My mother was more tolerant and did not cut my hair.

On Fridays, my mother would send me to the lending library, (there was no public library in our town), to pick up a book that she had reserved. After the meal, when the dishes were washed and put away, my mother would relax on the kitchen sofa (my bed) and read. I loved to snuggle up next to her, and read or daydream.

Washdays were a monthly affair lasting for three days. First the clothes were soaked overnight, next the white laundry was boiled in large kettles on the stove, then it was scrubbed and rinsed and soaked again overnight with a bluing agent and with starch. The laundry was then hung in the attic to dry and then the ironing began. The live coals heating the iron had to be replenished frequently with embers from the stove. This long and laborious process rendered the laundry wonderfully white and starched.

On summer days after school I used to play volleyball with my friends; I was pretty good at it and I loved the game. My brother played soccer and followed avidly the games of the local Jewish Makkabi team as well as the national and international soccer tournaments. He also loved music and he and my father played flute duets. I remember falling asleep on many evenings, listening to my father's playing. He had a wooden flute with an ivory mouthpiece. My father had great hopes in developing Julek's musical abilities. Once, when Julek was still very young, my father took him to a concert in Lwow, the largest city in our area. Julek was fascinated by the music and afterwards tried to imitate the conductor. My father was convinced that he was a budding musician of great talent. Perhaps he could have become one...

Shopping was a daily routine because of the lack of refrigeration. I used to accompany my mother to the open market where the peasants brought their produce for sale. Bargaining was standard procedure; one would inspect the chicken, cheese, or fruit, ask for the price and then walk over to the next stall to compare prices. After some bargaining, we walked home with baskets laden with produce. Canned or frozen foods were not available for purchase. Most housewives were very busy in the fall canning food. In our home, cucumbers and cabbage were pickled in large barrels and plum jam (povidla) was prepared in large copper kettles. We kids always managed to get in the way, but occasionally we helped to pit the plums. During those busy days, as the preparations for the winter were speeding up, we always had some women from the village help my mother. Large quantities of potatoes and other root vegetables were stored in the cellar. Long braids of garlic and onions were hung from the rafters. Sacks of flour and corn meal were stored in cool dry places, and large quantities of firewood were prepared for the cold winter months to come.

In fall, as our High Holidays approached, preparation for the Days of Awe began. It was customary to visit the cemetery before the holidays. My mother took me once with her to visit grandfather David Meltzer's grave. She placed a pebble on the gravestone, stroked the stone, prayed and cried. I learned that my grandfather David was a "Cohen" of the priestly caste. According to tradition, he was not buried in the cemetery proper but on the side, surrounded by a fence.

[Several years ago, I wandered in that desolate cemetery, searching for my grandfather's grave in vain. Most of the gravestones were removed by the Germans who paved their courtyards and sidewalks with them, only a few remain standing. I clutched tightly the stone in my hand, but found no gravestone to place it on...]

New Years and Yom Kippur (Day of Atonement) all Jewish businesses were closed. The whole community was praying in the great synagogue or in the many little houses of prayer that could be found on almost every street. Our family prayed in our Hebrew school, which was converted during the holidays into a house of worship.

On the Day of Atonement, my parents, like most other Jews spent the whole day at the synagogue, fasting and praying. I remember especially the last service in 1939, when black clouds were gathering on the horizon. The congregation's prayers were intermingled with much crying, as if they had a premonition of things to come.

As fall turned to winter, the temperatures often dropped below zero. Snow covered the garden and I had to wade knee-deep in the snow to make my way to school. Girls did not wear slacks in those days. We had to wear wool stockings, which I hated because they itched. My beloved grandmother used to knit stockings and gloves for all her grandchildren. On some of the hottest summer days I would find her sitting with her basket of wool on the porch, the knitting needles clicking as she made one more pair of gloves or stockings for a grandchild. I felt really grown up when she knitted for me my first pair of gloves with fingers. Nevertheless, I had frostbites on my fingers and toes almost every winter, because I loved to play in the snow.

The house was heated by wood-burning stoves, a large one in the kitchen, and a beautiful burgundy colored tile stove in the living room. On very cold days, my mother warmed our long winter underwear on the stove, to entice us to get out from under our warm feather comforters and brave the cold. The windows were covered with ice flowers and water froze in the vestibule when the fire died out and the temperature dropped at night. My mother used to get up at the crack of dawn to start the fire in the stove and prepare our breakfast.

On winter days, our usual breakfast consisted of hot cream of wheat and milk. Early in the morning, a peasant woman from the village used to bring fresh milk, which had to be boiled to pasteurize it. The more fat the milk contained, the more it was prized. When the milk was boiled, a thick skin formed on top. Most of my fussing in the morning was due to finding a bit of that skin in my milk. I hated it and I promised myself that when I grow up, I would never drink milk. Of course, I did not know then, that in a far-away country, which would become my home, milk comes in plastic containers and is served cold, without the hated thick skin on top of it. What a country!

There were no ready-made clothes available in our town. Getting a dress or a coat was a long and drawn-out process. One had to go to a store to buy the cloth and all the trimmings, then one found a seamstress (my aunt Zlata was one of the best in town) where one was measured, a paper pattern was made, and the cloth was cut and stitched together. Then there were several fittings until, finally, the dress was ready. We usually got a new outfit in the spring for Pesach (Passover) and new school clothes in the fall. My mother sewed beautifully and made many of my dresses. Of course, we did not have the closets full of clothes the way children have today. The usual wardrobe consisted of one good dress for holidays and special occasions, one or two dresses for every day, and a couple of skirts and blouses. Every bit of material was saved. A worn coat was taken apart, turned inside out and made into a dress or skirt for a child. Nothing was wasted, since it was difficult to make ends meet.

In 1937 my brother Julek applied for admission to the "gymnasium" (high school). He studied very hard all summer for the entrance exams. What amazed me was that he had to pass an exam in Latin, which was not taught in the public schools. He had private tutors and exams, both written and oral, lasted a few days. Even though my brother was a very good student, my parents were nervous. Each morning, the names of the students who had passed the exams on the previous day were posted on the wall. We all crowded around the board, and to my parents' great relief my brother's name appeared one morning. He was now officially a "gymnaziast", a high school student. My parents found a tailor to sew his prescribed navy blue uniform, with stripes on the sides of his pants. He looked so splendid in his new uniform and neat cap with the school emblem on it.

My father did not earn very much. There were constant worries in our house of how to pay for the Hebrew school and the "gymnazium" (high school) and still save enough money to be able to send my brother later to study abroad. My parents agonized about the growing anti-Semitism in Poland and hoped to be able to send my brother to study in England. Very few girls aspired to a higher education at that time. In my mother's family, only uncle Jacob had attended a university receiving a doctorate in chemistry. Her two sisters, Mincia and Zlata, completed high school and my mother attended a teachers' seminary in Zaleszczyki. She taught only for a very short time, because it was difficult for a Jew in Poland to get a government job. When she completed her studies, the only job she could get was teaching in some remote village, where most the peasants were not interested to have their children educated, since they needed them to help on the farm. Very few peasants in our region could read or write; only the priest and a few other men were literate.

On many a Saturday we assembled at my grandmother's house, the adults were sitting in the living room at grandmother's large table covered with a festive green plush tablecloth, sipping tea and talking. Very often the conversation turned to their experiences during World War I. I heard stories about the Cossacks burning, looting and raping women, and about the family's escape to Vienna. I was fascinated with the story of how they had smeared my mother's face with charcoal, to make her look ugly, so the Cossacks would not be after her. They surely had a difficult task since she was a beautiful young girl. The Vienna stories sent mixed messages: sometimes, they spoke of the joy of discovering that beautiful city, about the Prater and the Vienna Woods, but they also spoke of the hunger and the hardships they endured. They recalled with sadness their return home, only to find their house burned. They had to start rebuilding their home and their lives again. My grandfather built his house himself. Being quite artistic, he decorated the ceiling with beautiful medallions and painted birds on the veranda walls. All the cousins usually assembled on the large back porch, munching "kichlech" (cookies) that my grandmother used to bake for the Sabbath. The girls sang songs and teased one another. They loved to comb my long blond hair and put it up in fancy braids. The girls always teased my brother and his friends for being infatuated with a girl called Blanka, their schoolmate and the daughter of a well-known doctor in town. The boys used to serenade Blanka under her window. Lusiek played the violin and my brother the flute but, it seemed, they did not capture her heart.

In the summer of 1937, a municipal olympic size swimming pool was built in our town. A lovely large garden with many benches surrounded the pool. Jewish children could only look at the pool with envy from afar because a sign proclaimed that Jews and dogs were not allowed in the pool. We would stroll in the park, listen to the music, and watch young people dance and swim while feeling quite dejected ourselves. The monies to build this pool came from taxes levied on all the citizens, including Jews.

My father was a typical European man of his time; he never did any manual work around the house. One morning I saw a most unusual sight: my father with a bucket of water and a brush in his hand. He was trying to erase graffiti from the wall of our house, "Precz z Zydami" (Out with the Jews), before we children woke up since he did not want us to see it. He was not successful, no matter how hard he tried, he could not obliterate it completely. In 1918, after spending a long time as an officer in the Austrian army in the trenches in Italy, he volunteered to fight with the newly formed Polish army under Marshal Josef Pilsudski. He believed that if the Jews helped in the fight for an independent Poland, they would enjoy full civil rights and anti-Semitism would disappear. What an impossible dream! In Poland there is anti-Semitism even now without Jews. Some people thought it had been a foolish thing to do, but he hated to admit that they were right.

Anti-Semitism was intensifying in Poland. In the universities a "numerus clausus", was established, which allowed only a limited number of Jews to enter colleges and universities. Those Jewish students who were admitted were required to sit in the back rows, but most preferred to stand during the lectures. Incidents of violence were reported. Many of our young people studied abroad, especially in Czechoslovakia, Italy, and England.

A law was passed in parliament prohibiting the Jewish ritual slaughter of cattle and this brought great distress to many Orthodox Jews. My grandmother, who was strictly "kosher" (adhered to the proscribed dietary rules), refused to eat any meat from cattle not slaughtered in accordance with traditional laws.

My grandmother Zirl Meltzer, lived with my aunt Zlata and her daughter in the house my grandfather had built. Aunt Zlata was divorced, having been married in Vienna during the war. Zlata's daughter Wisia was a very pretty and gifted girl who wanted to become a dress designer. Grandmother was an orthodox lady who wore a "shaytel" (wig). She taught us children that the fundamentals of our faith, charity and kindness to others, should be shown by example, not by preaching. On Friday afternoons she always prepared part of a Sabbath meal for the family of a poor shoemaker, who lived in a tiny apartment on her property. She often sent me over with the Sabbath meal, a bit of Chalah and some cookies for the children. There were many children in that family and they lived in great poverty.

On Saturdays, she always sat with her prayer book in her hands as she greeted her children and grandchildren. I don't know how old she was when she was murdered, to me she always seemed old and fragile and very wise. She suffered from asthma and I remember her sitting on the edge of her bed, holding a hot little flat stone, on which some powder was smoldering while she inhaled the smoke that helped her breath. Her back was bent and she walked with a cane, yet in times of crisis she was the towering strength for the whole family. She was unquestionably the matriarch of the family. Her children loved and respected her very much.

Aunt Zlata was a very fine seamstress and many women in town came to her to have their dresses made. Her customers sat in the little entrance hall and studied carefully the latest fashion magazines from Paris. After they selected an outfit, my aunt would advise them what fabric to buy. Then came endless fitting sessions until the dress fitted perfectly. Several apprentices were working for my aunt and I liked to hang around and listen to their singing while they worked. In our electronic age, singing while you work has vanished. The shop was also a treasure trough for me, since I was allowed to pick lovely scraps of fabric for my only doll's dresses. Much later I wondered whether my granddaughter, who at last count amassed over one hundred "beanie babies", found greater enjoyment then I did with my little rag doll.

Two houses down Strzelecka Street lived my mother's youngest sister Mincia with her husband Nathan and their three children Bella, Max and Wisia. My uncle had a horse-driven oil press and peasants from nearby villages brought their sunflower seeds to be pressed into oil. I liked to observe this operation, but I felt sorry for my uncle's horse walking with his eyes covered round and round in a circle and turning the shaft that caused the heavy millstone to press the oil out of the seeds. The golden liquid flowed and filled one can after another in rapid succession. My uncle's work clothes glistened with oil and his face with sweat. He did not earn much for this hard labor and the family struggled to pay the high school tuition for their oldest daughter Bella and for the many medical expenses for little Wisia who was a deaf-mute child. They had traveled to Vienna to see a specialist who taught her sign language.

My mother's brother, Uncle Jacob, worked in Leipzig, Germany, as a chemist. He used to come every year to Horodenka for a visit. All my cousins and I looked forward to his visits, not only because he always brought us nice presents, but also because he really tried to get to know us. He was a bachelor who seemed to enjoy spending time with his nephews and nieces. One big irritant for him were the constant efforts of his mother and sisters to find him a wife. With the help of matchmakers, they arranged many meetings with eligible young women. Once, he got really upset and announced that if they do not stop arranging these "blind" dates, he would never come home again. This must have worked because from then on they left him alone.

We used to assemble at grandmother's house whenever his letters arrived and they were read and reread many times. The family's concern increased with the worsening situation for Jews in Germany. My parents were shocked to read about the annexation of Austria by Germany in March 1938. For them it was especially painful to see pictures of the jubilant crowds greeting Hitler in Vienna. Shortly thereafter, Germany annexed the Sudetenland and afterward the remainder of Czechoslovakia, but there was no jubilation in Prague. The family pleaded with my uncle to leave Germany immediately, but he wrote that his boss, though he was a Nazi, liked him and had promised to protect him. But he did not protect him when on October 27, 1938, the Gestapo showed up at my uncle's apartment and forced him and 18,000 other Jews who were Polish citizens to leave Germany immediately. They were brutally driven across the Polish border into a no-man's-land. Initially, the Polish government refused their entry into Poland, saying they did not need more Jews. These refugees were kept in an internment camp in Zbaszyn in appalling conditions, but after many months they were allowed to enter Poland. The family was relieved that he finally escaped Hitler's clutches.

My uncle eventually settled in Warsaw. He opened with a partner a factory for dyeing the pelts of domestic foxes to make them look like silver foxes, which were very fashionable at that time. This work was very similar to the work he had done in Leipzig.

The news about the Kristallnacht (Night of Broken Glass) that occurred in Germany on November 9, 1938 caused shock and disbelief. How could such brutality orchestrated by the government take place in a civilized country?

Jews in our town belonged to all kinds of political factions. There were those who looked to the east, believing in the promises of freedom and equality proclaimed by the Bolshevik Revolution. Most of these communists had been imprisoned and persecuted in pre-World War II Poland. Some lived to experience the bitter disillusionment when, after the Red Army marched into our town, they saw communism in practice. There were also Zionists of every stripe, from left to right, in our town. They "fought" (verbally) and debated about the political structure of a country that did not yet exist! But the dream to have a piece of land of their own and of the return to Zion burned deeply in many hearts. My mother was active in "Wizo" - The World International Zionist Organization. Polish kids would yell at us on occasion "go to Palestine", something that for many of us was an ardent wish. In every house there was a "pushka", a little blue and white box of the Jewish National Fund, into which Jews used to place a few "groshe" (pennies) for the purchase of land in Palestine. A messenger from Palestine would periodically collect the monies and bring news of progress in that far-away ancestral land.

Some religious Jews in our town vehemently opposed Zionism. They placed their hopes in a messianic redemption, preaching that only prayer and good deeds will hasten the coming of the Messiah.

My father, disillusioned with the policies of the Polish government and concerned by the frequent anti-Semitic incidents throughout Poland, encouraged my brother to join a Zionist youth group. In preparation for the hoped-for emigration to Palestine, the boys and the girls in the Zionist Youth Groups tried to learn to work the land. Others tried to find manual work during the summer, something that was not customary among our socially stratified society. My brother got a job cleaning the huge vats in the local sugar factory. Some people reproached my parents for allowing my brother to do this dirty work and to walk around in his soiled work clothes.

The Gathering Storm

In the summer of 1939, my brother Julek went to a Zionist camp (Ha'noar Ha'zioni) in the Carpathian Mountains. I was quite jealous, also wanting to go, but was told that I was too young. My parents promised that next year I should also go.

That summer, my mother, grandmother, aunt Zlata, cousin Wisia and I, went for vacation to Delatin, a small resort town in the Carpathian Mountains, close to my brother's camp. Father stayed home to work, since there were no paid vacations then. One day we visited my brother's camp. There were tents erected, as far the eye could see, and boys and girls in their blue and white uniforms strolled around. Blue and white Zionist flags fluttered in the breeze. Who could have foreseen, that these vibrant young people would be brutally murdered in just a few short years?

We took long walks in the beautiful woods and I played and splashed in the cold mountain brook near the little house my family had rented. We ate some of our meals in a restaurant and that was a big treat for me, since we never ate out. I was so happy during that summer, so totally unaware that we stood on the brink of an abyss.

A telegram arrived from my father during the second week of August, urging us to return home on the first available train. My mother woke me up at night, we dressed and left before sunrise. On the way to the railroad station, we stopped at a small grocery store. My mother managed to wake up the grocer and we bought some provisions for our journey. There was not much in that little store and I saw her do the unthinkable: buy cookies and candies and whatever else was available, since it was too early for the bread delivery and there was none left in the store. It crossed my mind that the war that everyone was now expecting could not be so bad after all, since it started with all those goodies.

The mobilization of the Polish army had already started. At every railroad station we saw troops moving west, to the German border. We did not know at the time that a great number of German troop trains were moving east with slogans like "We are off for Poland to thrash the Jews" scribbled on the cars. Hundreds of miles from my little town of Horodenka, plans were being set in motion to destroy and annihilate all we cherished and loved.

The trip home was uneventful. I munched the sweets and watched the troubled faces of the adults around me without much comprehension of what lay ahead.

When we got home, we learned about the German ultimatum and that full mobilization had been decreed. My father and my brother, one too old the other too young for military duty, were mobilized for civil defense. They walked around in steel helmets patrolling the streets. One of their duties was to make sure that all the windows were covered. They helped to build trenches in which to hide in case of air attacks. On the outskirts of town, fields were leveled to build an airstrip. We children were bringing drinking water for the workers. For a short while it appeared that all the people in town had a common goal: to fight the enemy. We did not anticipate that while our town people struggled to build an airstrip, almost the entire Polish air force would be destroyed on the ground, just a few days later. In spite of all the activities around us, my friends and I were getting ready for the new school year. I ran around town buying second-hand books (textbooks were not free in Poland) from those children who had a reputation of being good and neat students. I had all my books for the fifth grade and couldn't wait for school to start.

War Breaks out

On September 1, 1939, Germany attacked Poland, and now we were at war. Preparations started in earnest and many people were concerned that the Germans would use poison gas. Each household had to prepare some kind of a liquid concoction and we were instructed to dip cotton into this liquid and breathe through it in case of a gas attack. I shall never forget what happened when the first test alarm sounded: my mother covered the windows with pillows, as instructed, but she got caught in the curtains, spilled the special liquid and when the "all clear" was sounded she sat on the floor crying and laughing at the same time. I think she realized, perhaps for the first time, how vulnerable we all were and how pathetic our defenses stacked up against that mighty terror sweeping our country.

One morning, a real air attack took place. We were awakened early in the morning by the sound of sirens. We ran out in our nightclothes and jumped into the trench that my father and brother had dug in our garden. I could hear the whistle of the bombs and suddenly jumped out of the trench and ran home. After the all clear was sounded, my parents took me to task for disobeying instructions. I remember trying to explain to them that I did not want to be buried alive. If I had to, I wanted to die looking at the sky. I had to promise though that I shall never do it again.

There were some casualties in town, though most of the bombs fell into a pond. People thought that the bombs were directed at the large sugar factory nearby, but the Germans had mistaken the shimmering waters of the pond for the tin roof of the factory. One young Jewish boy was killed, and it was told that his father refused any help and carried him in his arms to the Jewish cemetery where he buried him.

We began to see refugees in our town from all over Poland. We were close to the Romanian border and many people, among them high government officials and other dignitaries, were fleeing to Romania. The townspeople offered food and shelter to the refugees. We heard that the Jewish owner of a book store in the center of town offered assistance to some refugees but was stunned to be asked if he was a Jew. Some Polish refugees declined help from Jewish people. Even then, in their darkest hour of defeat, some of the Poles did not forget their vicious anti-Semitism.

My parents also considered fleeing to Romania, but they worried whether they would be able to take care of the family in a strange land. They remembered only too well their plight as refugees during World War I. After much discussion, it was decided that my father and my brother should go across the border. We had heard that in Germany Jewish men were taken to slave labor camps, but everyone thought that women and children would be safe. Not in our worst nightmares could we have imagined what was to come. There were no prophets of old to warn us of the impending catastrophe.

After much soul searching my parents decided not to split the family and to await our fate together. Strong and enduring family bonds had been our strength in the past, but now the unwillingness to separate doomed us all for destruction.

We heard about the German claims that their attack on Poland was in reprisal for an alleged attack by Polish troops on the radio station in Gleiwitz, but nobody believed this. Many years later, after this war had claimed millions of lives and brought destruction over most of Europe, did the world learn about this deception. It turned out that the purported Polish attack in Gleiwitz had actually been staged by the Germans. They shot some prisoners, dressed them in Polish uniforms and placed their bodies at the radio station.

The news from the front was getting worse, day-by-day. Warsaw, as well as many other Polish cities, were bombed repeatedly. The fleeing refugees were often machine-gunned from the air. My uncle Jacob was among those who fled from Warsaw. Once again, he was on the run from the Germans, but no matter how fast he ran, he could not outrun the Nazi terror.

My uncle finally reached Horodenka. He described the mayhem and the horror the fleeing refugees had endured, but my parents could not believe that civilians were fired upon. Their frame of reference was World War I, which they remembered mainly as a trench war. The civilians in the rear of the frontlines were safe. After all, did not the Geneva Convention forbid harming civilians? They had yet to learn not to expect any civilized behavior from the new barbarians who came from the heart of Europe, not from some remote jungle. A new word entered our vocabulary: Blitzkrieg. The German army seemed unstoppable as they conquered one city after another. On September 3rd, when France and England declared war against Germany, our hopes were raised for a while, but the reality on the ground did not change.

There was sudden rejoicing in our town when a young Pole raced on a motorcycle through town yelling that he had seen Polish soldiers on Soviet tanks. We all thought that the Russians had come to the aid of Poland, but sadly, the opposite was true: Poland had been stabbed in the back and was once again divided and occupied by foreign powers. The news of the Hitler-Stalin pact was a severe blow to our expectations.

The Russians Are Coming

Within days, Red Army tanks appeared in the city streets and the Soviet occupation began. As these rumbling giants drove passed on our narrow street, our house shook, windows rattled and one wall of our house cracked. The soldiers did not seem threatening, they even tried to project friendliness, especially towards children.

The Russians treated Polish soldiers as prisoners of war and kept them under guard in my school, next door to our house. Julek and I were hanging on the fence and talking with them. Some soldiers threw money from the windows and asked us to buy cigarettes for them, which we did. For a while, the Russian guards allowed us to do that, but after a few days, strange-looking soldiers from Central Asia arrived. They pointed their guns at us and motioned us to leave.

The people in town organized a soup kitchen. They set up huge copper kettles in our garden and prepared food for the prisoners. A few days later, we watched with sadness as they were marched through the town holding up their trousers since their belts had been taken from them. We never learned what happened to these officers and soldiers and years later I wondered whether they were among those massacred by the Soviets in the Katyn forest.

There was a lot of confusion in town, not only because we did not understand the Russian language; their whole political system was foreign to us. Political indoctrination began almost immediately at work and in school. My father raged against the Soviets which frightened my mother very much and she tried to calm him down as best she could. The fear of imprisonment and of Siberian exile was always with us.

Within weeks, the schools reopened. Some teachers were brought in from the USSR. Coeducational schools were new to us. In pre-war Poland, boys and girls attended separate elementary schools. We were assigned to a Ukrainian school where the language of instruction was Ukrainian but there was a heavy emphasis on Russian language studies. My parents were not thrilled with this turn of events, and they tried to get permission to establish a Yiddish school in our town. I remember going with my mother and other parents and children to petition the Soviet superintendent of schools to allow us to open a Yiddish school. Permission was granted and a Yiddish school with grades one through four was indeed opened. My mother taught in that school, but I could not attend it, since I was already a fifth grader. My mother and all other teachers were compelled to study the Constitution of the USSR, as well as the writings of Lenin and Stalin and she struggled with that late into the night.

For me, the changes from the Polish school were not entirely unwelcome. The new masters preached equality of all peoples and nations, which sounded good. Anti-Semitic slurs were strictly forbidden. All children were to be treated equally, or almost equally, the children of poor peasants and artisans becoming the elite, while those whose parents were formerly well off were not always treated kindly.

Portraits of Lenin and Stalin adorned the classroom walls and we sat under their watchful and "benevolent" gaze. We were told that we lived in the best of all possible worlds, yet the reality on the ground was quite different. Large posters with political slogans that we did not quite understand crowded every wall. The best students were urged to join the "Pioneers", a communist youth group. I was also invited to join, but I could not understand why my father was not thrilled at all when I showed up with a red kerchief around my neck. I thought he should be proud of me, after all, wasn't this an indication of my scholarship? The authorities took over a very nice villa of a former wealthy family and established there a Pioneers' club. Games and books were available there for us, and we participated in many organized activities that I enjoyed. The game of chess was especially encouraged. Libraries in Poland before the war were not free, so having access to a variety of books was a joy. We were too young to understand the political agenda and the propaganda contained in many of the stories that we read.

Shortages of all kinds began to appear. Due to a lack of fuel, the classrooms were poorly heated and most of the time we sat in class wearing our coats and gloves. Paper was also in short supply and the Soviet notebooks we received were made of very coarse paper on which the ink spread in messy blotches. I had to redo many homeworks since my mother did not accept any excuses, but, I guess, she also commiserated with us.

We were often told that the Soviet Union had many enemies who try to infiltrate across the borders and harm the people. All children had to attend paramilitary drills. We marched with wooden rifles, staged mock battles in which we stormed some snow-covered hills outside of town. I found this to be much fun, but my parents thought it was an inappropriate political indoctrination of children.

My uncle Jacob who had moved to Horodenka had married a woman from Vilna. My new aunt Gita was a dentist and she spoke Russian very well, which was of great help later when my uncle got in trouble with the Soviet authorities. He had received a "bad" passport (internal identification document) from the Soviets because he was considered politically unreliable, having co-owned a factory before the war. He was told that he could not remain in our town, and was threatened with exile to Siberia. The family was desperate but his wife intervened with the authorities and pleaded for him. To everyone's great relief, his passport was exchanged for a "good" one, allowing him to live and work in Horodenka. He opened the only medical laboratory in town. Ironically, exile to Siberia might have saved his life.

A simple-minded water carrier named Myku lived in our town. He had a clubfoot and one could hear him from far away stomping heavily as he carried pails of water that hung from a yoke on his shoulders. Friday afternoons, he made the rounds of Jewish households for a "n'duve", an alm of a few groshens, for his Sabbath meal. One afternoon he came to our house and my mother told him not to go across the street to the Szpirer family because they had been arrested the night before and sent to Siberia. Myku, in his innocence, made a prophetic prediction: "If they took a rich man like Szpirer to Siberia it must be good there". People laughed and repeated his "foolish" words. Yet, in a way, he was right; Siberia was certainly preferable to the horror that befell our town a short time later and some of those deported survived the war.

We began to experience shortages and rationing. One that was very difficult for my father was the lack of cigarettes. In World War I, in the trenches in Italy he became addicted to smoking, not aware of the health hazard this entailed. When cigarettes were not available, he managed to buy loose tobacco and my brother and I would spend many hours filling cigarette hulls with tobacco. He could not stand the coarse "makhorka" tobacco that the Russians rolled in newspaper and smoked. In the beginning, the local merchants were very happy when the Russians bought everything in sight. They quickly found out, however, that one could not buy much with the rubles they received and that it was not possible to replenish the merchandise. Whenever something was sold in a store, long lines immediately formed. One bought whatever was available and in the largest quantities permitted. It did not matter that one did not need galoshes size 13 because one could always barter them for something useful. Staying in line became a full-time job, just to be able to provide for the family.

My father continued to work at the flourmill that was now nationalized, as were many other enterprises and stores in town, and a Russian supervisor was brought in.

Most of the Russian teachers were friendly. We were introduced for the first time to Russian literature, poetry and music, and found them to be very beautiful. Some of the Russian soldiers, my parents thought, were rather primitive. The authorities requisitioned one room in our house and billeted three soldiers there. One of the officers was a "politruc", a political commissar who was an intelligent person, but after a short while he was sent to the Finnish front. He had many discussions with my father and he predicted that the war in Europe would end in 1945. We were shocked, how could one endure war for such a long duration, and indeed very few of us did. Eventually, two of the officers left, and one of them brought his wife to live with him. They shared our kitchen and we soon discovered how communism worked in practice: they simply helped themselves to anything they pleased, which greatly irritated my mother.

Fear gripped many people as the deportations to Siberia became more frequent. We heard the rumble of trucks in the night and entire families were taken away. There were no trials, people simply vanished. Many former political and religious leaders, both Poles and Jews, as well as wealthy people were exiled to Siberia. We learned that receiving a letter from America made one suspect. To have belonged to a Zionist organization was dangerous. One never quite knew what made one undesirable or suspect under this regime. People lived in fear, while we children were being taught that we lived in the best of all possible worlds, under the great and wise leadership of Stalin.

We were told, for example, about the great courage and heroism of a young boy, Pavlik Morozov, who had informed the police on his father. His father was a Kulak (wealthy peasant) who hid grain to avoid turning it over to the state during the great collectivization in Russia in the thirties. We were taught that loyalty to the state came before family solidarity. My parents were dismayed, they knew that millions of Russian farmers had been starved to death by Stalin in order to build the "Kolkhoz" (collective farm system). When my parents realized what we were taught, they were stunned and became more cautious in discussing things in front of their children.

The first of May was celebrated in grand style during the Soviet rule. All workers were required to march in the parades, carrying banners extolling communism, and pictures of Lenin and Stalin were everywhere. All marchers assembled at the soccer stadium for patriotic speeches, music and dancing. All schools participated in the festivities and a classmate and I were chosen to be the lead couple in a traditional Ukrainian dance to be performed at the stadium. I ran to my Ukrainian schoolmate across the street and borrowed one of her beautiful costumes, lots of colorful beads, a beautifully embroidered blouse and a long skirt. I am sure the political speeches and slogans were of no interest to me, it was just fun to be with my friends and dance.

At War Again

As the summer of 1941 approached, I looked forward to a summer vacation and I hoped to be able to go to a sleep away camp that the Soviets had established for Pioneers. Fate took a different turn: on June 22, 1941, the Germans attacked the Soviet Union and once again we were at war.

The Soviets had always bragged about the invincibility of the Red Army. So it was a shock to see how quickly their defenses crumbled. We saw the "Blitzkrieg" in action, again. We were pretty much cut off from the world, yet news trickled in from time to time about the situation in German occupied Poland. We heard about German atrocities against the defenseless civilian population and especially about the brutal treatment of the Jews. Some people in our town, even those without any communist leanings, tried to flee with the Russians. The situation was chaotic but my father detested the communist regime and decided not to leave.

There were some battles in our town with casualties on both sides. A number of civilians were also killed. We had just left grandmother's house when on the way home the shelling started. Bullets were flying everywhere and, unable to reach our house, we found shelter overnight with a Jewish family and walked home the next morning. On our way home, I saw for the first time the horrors of war: a dead young Soviet soldier was lying on the sidewalk, as if asleep, with his knees pulled up to his chest. I was shocked seeing a dead person for the first time, especially one so young! Little did I know that in the months and years to come, death would be such a close companion and the shock would wear off before long. I thought about his mother, who did not yet know that her son was dead and I grieved for both. During the battle in our town there were also a number of civilian casualties.

By the end of June the Soviet troops withdrew. On July 4, 1941, Hungarian troops occupied our town. The Ukrainian nationalists welcomed them with bread and salt, as is the custom among those people. During the few days of "interregnum", the local Ukrainian thugs killed many Jews in outlying villages. News reached us of the pogroms in the cities of Przemysl and Lwow, where many Jews were killed. We were shocked to hear that in the neighboring village of Niezwisk, Ukrainian peasants under the leadership of their priest Golduniak rounded up some 200 Jews. They kept them in the cellar of the local school bound with barbed wire, then forced them onto a ferry and threw them into the Dniester river. Fear gripped our community and young Jews organized self-defense groups. Some leaders of the Jewish community approached the priest of the Horodenka Ukrainian church and asked him to intervene with the Ukrainian police to stop their brutal behavior toward the Jews. In his next sermon the priest reminded his congregants that in 1919, the Poles first started pogroms against the Jews, but eventually they also murdered Ukrainians. He pleaded with them not to harm the Jews.

At first, some Jews thought that it was better to have Hungarian troops, rather than German, occupy our city, hoping that they would behave more humanely, but that notion was soon dispelled. One Hungarian lieutenant named Simon distinguished himself in his brutal behavior towards the Jews. He ordered some 70 Jews to repair the bridge over the Dniester River near Siemakowce, but he mistreated them brutally. His dog was trained to attack them and many were injured. He also amused himself by forcing Jews to sing Yiddish songs and dance for him.

Three Hungarian officers were billeted in my grandmother's house. They amused themselves by shooting at the ceiling or unleashing their vicious dogs on innocent people. My mother's cousin, Vovek Friedman, was mauled quite badly by their dogs. In the middle of July, the Hungarians established a Judenrat (Jews' Council) in town, with the lawyer Alfred Merbaum chosen against his will to be the head. On July 31 an order was issued that by August 1 all Jews must wear a yellow armband on their left arm.

We began to see Hungarian Jews and Jews from Podkarpacka Rus (formerly part of Czechoslovakia) being driven through our town. The Hungarians had expelled thousands of Jews. Some of them were transported by railroad and trucks, but those from the villages often drove their horse drawn buggies. Many had been driven on foot for days, young and old, men, women and children. These people were in a most deplorable condition. The townspeople tried to help, providing shelter for the night and food and water for the journey. These poor people were strictly forbidden to remain in town. Some of the desperate parents among them left their infant children behind with the Jewish community. An orphanage was established and Zionist youth groups cared for these children.

We soon learned about the fate of these unfortunate people: the end of August they, along with many local Jews, were all shot in the vicinity of Kamieniec Podolski. Between 12,000 and 18,000 Jews were massacred.

The Beginning of Nazi Terror

In July 1941, the Germans occupied our town and the reign of terror began. One of the first things they did was to erect eight gallows as a warning to what would happen to anyone who did not follow their orders. They proceeded to desecrate the main synagogue in town; they dragged the rabbi out of his house, beat him mercilessly and demanded that he dance for them. They destroyed the ark and burned the Torah scrolls and prayer books. The first Gestapo chief, Obersturmführer Doppler, was a vicious anti-Semite. He was succeeded by Kreishauptmann (district chief) Hans Hag. Hag was an SS-man who managed to exceed his predecessor in brutality and greed. He continually demanded money, gold, and other valuables from the "Judenrat".

The chief military officer, a Mr. Fiedler from Berlin, turned out to be an anti-Nazi. He was, supposedly, overheard saying that if Germany wins the war, he would shoot himself. Fiedler behaved decently, and on occasion warned the Jewish community of impending "akcias" (the roundup of Jews for deportations and mass murder). He frequently visited a young Jewish woman who lived across the street from us, ignoring the fact that socializing with Jews was strictly forbidden.

Day after day, new orders were issued, each one more vicious and distressing than the one before, all providing for the death penalty, if not obeyed.

For example:

All Jewish men from ages 14 to 60 must register for forced labor.

All Jews must wear a white armband with a blue Star

of David on the right arm above the elbow

Jewish children cannot attend school.

Jews cannot socialize with Christians.

Jews cannot work for Christians or Christians for Jews.

All Jewish businesses and factories must be handed over to the Germans

Jewish doctors and lawyers are forbidden to practice their professions.

All radios, gold, silver, furs, etc. must be turned over to the Germans authorities.

If any German set his sight on anything, your house, your apartment, your furniture, paintings, or any other valuables, it was his to take.

The greatest government-sponsored robbery and thievery in history was taking place in broad daylight!

My parents remembered the terror of the Cossacks when they invaded their little town during World War I, but they expected a more humane behavior from a western "civilized" nation. They were steeped in German literature and culture and were stunned and totally unprepared for the viciousness and the terror of the German occupation.

When the call to register for forced labor was issued, everyone tried to find a job in town since they feared being sent away to one of the notorious labor camps. Initially, people registered for work voluntarily, but when word got out about the horrible conditions in these camps, people refused to go and went into hiding. Periodically, the police swept through the ghetto in search for eligible men.

My father and my brother registered for work. My father was assigned to his former job as an accountant in the flourmill because they could not find an Aryan to take his place. My brother's work assignments varied: he had to pave the German commandant's courtyard with tombstones from the Jewish cemetery and he also worked in the garage of the German commandant keeping his fleet of cars in good repair.

If I could only paint my mother's strained face as she stood each evening at the window, peeking from behind the curtain, while waiting for their return! One never knew if they would come back or in what condition they might be. The men were often beaten at work, some were shot and many drowned building a bridge across the Dniester River.

The order to wear the armband with the Star of David was met with mixed emotions. We were quite apprehensive that this was a passport to death, but it was also a traditional symbol of our people and young girls lovingly embroidered armbands for their boyfriends. On occasion, if the armband slipped below the elbow, people were beaten and sometimes shot.

When schools reopened, I remember standing at the gate of our house, and watching my Aryan schoolmates pass on their way to school, some averting their eyes as they passed me, others with unfriendly expressions on their faces. I ran to my mother and asked why I could not go to school (I still asked WHY in those days), after all, I was a pretty good student and well behaved, I insisted. I shall never forget the pained expression in her eyes when she tried to console me. It must have been exceptionally difficult for her since she was a mother as well as a teacher prevented from doing what she loved so much.

When commercial activity resumed in town, not only were all Jewish stores taken over by Aryans, but Jews were not allowed to enter these stores. It became difficult to get provisions to feed the family. As long as we were in our home though, we did not lack too much. We had vegetables and fruits from the garden, some of the peasants still sold us milk, eggs and chickens. Only later, when we were shut in the ghetto, did the situation become very grave.

The order forbidding socializing between Christian and Jews hardly had any effect on us, since there had been very little of it even before the war. But the stigmatization and isolation of our people had a very negative effect and far-reaching consequences.

What was deeply disturbing was the order forbidding Jewish doctors to treat patients. Complications from malnutrition and the widespread epidemic of typhus caused great suffering among our people, while our doctors could only stand by, unable to offer any help to their patients. Of course, not even the simplest medicines were available in the ghetto.

As to lawyers, their services were certainly not in demand in the ghetto; these were lawless and brutal times. They must have wondered how justice under the occupiers had become so perverted. In Germany, lawyers had drafted the "Nuremberg Laws" and as judges they implemented some of the most unjust and corrupt laws in history!

The SS Death Head regiments followed closely behind the frontline troops. When my mother saw for the first time the crossbones and skull insignia on their hats and shoulder pads, she used a Hebrew expression that these men walked with the "malach ha'mavet" (the angel of death) on their arm. It was not very long before we experienced the full force of their brutality.

In our town there were also a number of Germans in the civilian administration but they all wore uniforms. My father's boss was a middle-aged man named Müller. Father used to tell us that he was not a bad guy. One evening, he appeared with his orderly at the door of our home. He sat down, took off his holster and gun and started talking with my parents. He seemed a bit drunk and my parents were terrified because a German was not allowed to socialize with Jews. As the evening progressed he became more aggressive and at one point he entered the room where I slept. As I woke up, I saw him standing over my bed, mumbling something in German that I did not understand. I was told later, that he called me "my blond angel". He then went into the kitchen, put a gun to my mother's head and demanded that she confess that "bei dieser ist ein Arier gewesen" (that an Aryan had fathered this one). My brother sneaked me out of the house and, in spite of the curfew, we ran quite terrified through back streets to my grandmother's house. I did not quite understand what was going on, I was more scared of the darkness than of the Germans. My parents did not tell me all the details about that harrowing night; after a while they managed, with the help of the German orderly, to get Herr Müller out of the house.

Much later, after the war, I have been criticized for using the word German rather than Nazi in my descriptions, but all I saw were Germans in uniforms. We had no way of knowing which one of them was a member of the Nazi party, but they were all Germans and all were a threat to our lives.

A few days after the excitement with Mr. Müller, I was playing with two of my cousins in our garden. We were shaking a plum tree and collecting the sweet plums, when we suddenly saw a German standing at the fence and motioning to us. We froze, not understanding what he wanted. He motioned to us that he wanted some plums. We gave him all our plums and ran away. We began to understand the danger each German posed for us, we just did not yet know that one could not run far enough or fast enough from their murderous grip. My two little cousins who picked plums with me on that day did not survive the war.

Ghettos, "Akcias" and the End of Jewish Horodenka

In October 1941, a Ghetto was established consisting of a few streets in the predominantly Jewish section of town. Barbed wire was strung across the street at the entrance to the ghetto that was patrolled by Jewish and Ukrainian police. We had to leave our house and move to my grandmother's house, which was inside the ghetto. A horse-drawn wagon pulled up into our yard and my parents put a few possessions on the wagon. We left a few things with our Ukrainian neighbor, but most of our furniture and other possession remained in the house. As the wagon began to pull away, I picked up my little white kitten to take along with me, but my mother told me to put her down because there wouldn't be enough food for pets in the ghetto. I was shocked, not enough food to feed a little kitten? What kind of a place is it going to be?

Our poor German shepherd fared much worse. His name was Adolph and we lived in terror that someone might inform the authorities of this great disrespect for the Führer. We gave him away immediately after the Germans entered our town.

We settled in one of the apartments in my grandmother's house. We had a large kitchen and a bedroom, quite a luxury in those days. Thousands of people were crammed into a few narrow streets, not only from all over town, but also from the outlying villages. The ghetto was closed, and only people who had work permits could get out.

I was happy to live again close to my best girlfriend Genia Reis who lived just a few houses away. After we settled in, my mother assembled a few of my friends and tried to run a little school for us, though that was forbidden under the penalty of death. In a windowless room we worked on the sixth grade curriculum, studying language, math, science as well as the history of our people. Later, I wondered whether my mother should have taught us how to make "Molotov cocktails"! Perhaps, she tried in the short time remaining to instill in us the importance of education, a pride in our heritage and the hope that some day this horror would pass and that the eternal ethical and moral values of our people would prevail. She tried desperately to keep our lives as normal as possible under difficult circumstances. Our "school" did not last long; it became increasingly dangerous to walk the city streets. My friends did not dare to come and one by one they disappeared.

The Germans decreed that a Judenrat (Jewish council) be established in the ghetto. Initially, the most respected people were chosen but they soon realized that the Germans were using them to compile the lists for forced labor and deportations and to pass on their orders and their continuous demands for money, gold, and other valuables. Few were eager to take on that task and most were forced to do it.

As winter approached, hunger began to be felt in the ghetto. One could not buy provisions in stores and the peasants were not allowed to enter the ghetto to sell their wares. The rations allotted to the Jews were extremely meager, 600 calories a day. Many years later I read in the diary of Hans Frank, the Governor General of Poland, that in August 1942, 1.2 million Jews had been condemned to death by starvation.

One started to see children with swollen stomachs begging in the streets of the ghetto. The community established a soup kitchen and young people from the Zionist youth groups helped to feed starving people. They also helped to take care of the children in the orphanage. Many of these brave young people perished with their charges shortly thereafter.

My father continued to work at the mill, so we had enough flour and could barter some of it for other food. My grandmother also established a soup kitchen. At first, only a few children came to the back door steps, but soon the line was getting longer and the soup was getting thinner.

Persecutions and indignities were perpetrated daily against our people. Orthodox Jews had their side locks ripped off, many people were beaten and some were shot. All businesses were confiscated, professional people could not work and slave laborers were not paid for their hard work. Hunger and diseases were rampant in the ghetto. People bartered their possessions for food. My father had a beautiful stamp collection that he also traded for food. It must have been very painful for him, since stamp collecting was his favorite hobby.

On calm days, when the weather permitted, all my cousins and some of their friends gathered on my grandmother's back porch. The girls embroidered the Star of David armbands for their boyfriends and romances flourished. Of course, the deteriorating situation in the ghetto was always the main topic of discussion. Suggestions were made and plans were hatched on how to escape from this hell. The news from the front was discouraging: the Germans seemed to be unstoppable, as they penetrated deep into Russia. My father was poring over an atlas trying to predict where the Russians would finally stop the German offensive; cities like Kiev, Gomel, Moghilev, Smolensk and Oriol were often named, but the Germans continued their advance. My father did not live to hear about the reversals and the decisive defeats of the Germans on the snow covered steppes of Russia and on the beaches of France.

Every rumor and every bit of news were seriously debated. Some of the more outrageous rumors, (or was it wishful thinking?) claimed that Hitler had died or that the Germans had rebelled against his tyranny. We were totally cut off from any news of the outside world. The German papers reported only great victories or successful strategic retreats.

When the order came to deliver to the Germans all gold, silver and furs, most people complied and brought their valuables to the Judenrat, but many hid some of their precious possessions. My grandmother refused to part with her silver Sabbath candlesticks. My father and my uncle built a wooden box, wrapped the candlesticks in waterproof material and buried them in the garden. In the darkness of night all the adults and children made their way quietly downstairs to the garden and watched as my uncle buried the box. We were all told, even the youngest amongst us, to remember the place, should one of us survive and be able to retrieve them.

[A few years ago my husband and I stood in that garden but, painfully, we realized that under the unstable conditions in that region, now part of the Ukraine, it would be impossible for us to retrieve the candlesticks. The Ukrainian government interdicted the removal of valuables from the country. I still hope that someday my children or grandchildren may be able to hold in their hands this precious relic from our former lives...]

I could not understand why the Germans needed my little rabbit fur muff and the fur collar of my winter coat but to my great dismay, my parents insisted that we follow orders and delivered them to the Germans. My mother made for me a new velvet collar for my coat, which looked quite nice, but I was angered every time I wore it. I wondered whether they hoped to keep warm during the Russian winter with the help of my fur muff?

Men were periodically caught on the streets and sent to concentration camps. The most feared concentration camp was the Janowska Lager in Lvov. Horrible stories of beatings, starvation, and executions reached us. At one such roundup, my father was also caught. As he stood in line, his German boss showed up and started cursing and kicking him while screaming "what are you doing here when I need you at work?" He got him out of the line and, for once, saved his life. Next day, this "savior" was given a beautiful hand-woven tapestry that used to hang on our wall.

I asked my father about his thoughts as he stood there in line facing death. He said that his eyes were fixed on the nice pair of boots on the guy in front of him and he thought he would have liked to have a pair like that. He obviously tried to make light of it and shield us from the devastating reality.

Toward the end of November, rumors reached our town of an impending "akcia". Kreishauptmann Hans Hag told the Judenrat, that if they would give him three kilograms of gold, some diamonds and other precious stones, he would see to it that nothing would happen to our people. The Judenrat was able to collect the required amount of gold and valuables and handed it over to him, in hopes of saving the community.

Friday, December 4, 1941, an order was issued that all Jews must assemble in front of the Great Synagogue to be inoculated against typhus. The Germans said that those who did not have a certificate of inoculation would loose their ration card and would not be allowed to remain in town. Some wondered why the Germans suddenly cared about our health. A prominent Jewish doctor in town assured everyone; he said that he had been ordered to assemble nurses to help him with the inoculation.

My father was skeptical and decided to hide us in the flourmill were he worked. Under the cover of darkness, we stole our way from the ghetto and reached our old house. My parents still had the keys to the house. We opened the kitchen door very quietly and entered. The place was empty and very cold. I remembered how warm and cozy the kitchen had once been; it was the place where the whole family assembled, while wonderful odors emanated from the large hearth, especially the smell of freshly baked "chalah" and sweet breads that my mother baked on Fridays. My heart ached for our shattered lives; we had to steal our way into our own house like thieves! In one part of the house lived some Ukrainian people whom we did not know and feared. The Germans had promised a pound of sugar and money for turning in a Jew, and many had accepted that offer. On the other side of the kitchen lived a Ukrainian man who knew my father and he tried to help. At night, as my parents, my brother and I lay huddled together on the bare kitchen floor, this man, whose name I don't remember, entered the kitchen and covered us all with a sheepskin coat. This simple act of compassion brought tears to my eyes, I could not fall asleep for a long time. Before dawn, we made our way through the back streets to the mill. My father hid us in a dark little nook on the second floor of the mill. As daylight broke, we heard shots and cries coming from the town. We huddled in the freezing cold, in great terror and agonized about the fate of our family and friends in the ghetto. The next day, we continued to lay very quietly behind the sacks of flour. The mill was in operation and we feared that workers might discover and denounce us to the Gestapo.

[Fifty-six years later, my husband and I visited Horodenka. We walked up the road to the mill that I knew so well. As we came closer, I recognized the familiar hum of the machinery. The place had hardly changed, but now the sacks of flour were being loaded onto trucks rather than horse-driven carts. I walked quickly to where my father's office had been, but the place now looked different: the original entrance door had been blocked off and replaced by a different one. This was, perhaps, symbolic: I could never enter through that door again and see my father sitting at his desk and smiling when he noticed me. I got permission to climb up to our former hiding place. The continuous and monotonous hum of the flour sifters transported me back to those terri-

ble days when my family and I were hiding there. The place looked the same, sacks of flour were stacked all around and flour-covered spider webs were everywhere. I could barely descend those narrow steps and keep my emotions in check in front of the crowd of curious workers that surrounded us.]

The following day, a Sunday, all seemed quiet and no more shots were heard. We made our way back to the ghetto; as we approached the area, cries and lamentations were heard from every house. It seemed no family had been spared. With our hearts beating fast, we entered my grandmother's house and found most of the family assembled there. They had been hidden in a bunker during the "akcia". Only my mother's younger sister, aunt Mincia had gone to the prescribed place, hoping to get the needed permit allowing the family to receive a "Kennkarte" (ID) for food rations and thus remain in town. My uncle Nathan and his children, Bella, Max, and Wisia were in tears since their mother never returned.

We found out that the "akcia" had lasted two days. As more and more people assembled at the synagogue, they were suddenly surrounded by the Gestapo, SS, and the Ukrainian police. They were then herded into the synagogue and kept there for two days without any food or water. Many people were severely beaten and some were shot. The Gestapo and their helpers swept through the ghetto with their dogs in search of more people. Their terrifying screams of "Juden raus" (Jews get out) were heard throughout the ghetto. On the third day, trucks drove up to the synagogue, the people were loaded unto the trucks and were driven away. Among them was my mother's youngest sister, our tall, beautiful redhead aunt Mincia. The whole family was in despair.

My sick and frail grandmother, still the pillar of strength throughout the whole ordeal, tried to calm everyone. She said that as soon as we find out where our people were taken, we would send to my aunt packages of food and warm clothing and, perhaps, we would succeed in buying her freedom and bring her home. We went to sleep somewhat consoled, only to wake up next morning and learn about the tragedy that had befallen our people.

Half of the town's Jewish population, 2500 men, women and children, were driven 12 km from Horodenka to Siemakowcze on the Dniester River. There they were forced to undress in a barn and then run in groups of five to an open pit were they were shot. One woman who was only wounded managed to make her way back to Horodenka and she related the horror she had seen. As music was blaring (to muffle the sound of the gun shots), and vodka was flowing, the Germans and their helpers took turns shooting these innocent men, women and children.

We also heard details about the horrible conditions the people in the synagogue endured for the two days preceding the massacre. People were passing out, children were crying. One woman tried to come closer to the door to help her fainting baby get a breath of air, but a German grabbed the baby from the mother's arms and smashed its head on the Holy Ark, and then shot the mother. The child's father, Mr. Liebmann, witnessed this horror and became paralyzed on the very spot.

During the "akcia" the Gestapo entered the Jewish orphanage. Eyewitnesses reported seeing how the Germans smashed some of the babies' heads on the walls and threw others from the second floor into street, where a truck collected them. When the "akcia" was over, our people found the little tables in the orphanage had been set up for breakfast with a slice of bread on each plate. The young people from the Zionist organization who took care of these children perished with their charges.

Most of the Jewish homes in the ghetto had a yellow poster attached to the door, letting the Gestapo know that this house was searched and all the Jews taken away. Those who survived were not allowed to enter their homes. They had to register with the Judenrat again. The Gestapo kept tabs on the number of survivors in preparing for the next "akcia".

After the "akcia", the Gestapo chief Doppler came to the Judenrat and demanded 2500 Marks as payment for the bullets used to kill the Jews. He prohibited any public expressions of mourning and ordered all men to shave and go to work "as usual". (Jewish custom prohibits shaving during the "Shiva" period, the seven days of mourning.)

[Fifty-six years after the massacre, my husband and I visited Siemakowce. As we approached the place, the road narrowed and was barely passable by car. The mass grave was largely overgrown with trees and shrubs. Nearby stood a monument, erected during the Soviet rule with the inscription "To the Victims of Fascism". On a tablet subsequently added by survivors from Israel, inscriptions in Hebrew, Yiddish, Ukrainian and English read: "Mass grave of 2500 Jews, adults and children, from Horodenka and vicinity who were murdered here by Nazis on December 4, 1941. May the memory of the Holocaust victims be blessed forever". I lit a memorial candle and my husband recited the Kaddish, the mourner's prayer, though I found it difficult to extol God's name in this place. I placed a pebble on the mass grave, an ancient Jewish custom, and walked back to the car shattered by the memory of what had happened here to my people.]

As the terrible news spread through the ghetto, deep despair overwhelmed everyone. Some people, mostly the young ones, tried to flee across the border to Romania. We heard later that many were caught by the Romanian border police who turned them over to the Gestapo and they were shot at the border.

Several people committed suicide. Next door to grandmother's house lived a childless middle-aged couple. One morning, both were found dead by poisoning. Some tried to acquire Aryan birth certificates and baptismal documents and hide out as Christians outside the ghetto. Many tried to find a hiding place with a friendly Christian family, but few succeeded. Everyone built some kind of bunker (hiding place): some were most elaborate underground chambers equipped with provisions for a long-term stay, other were hideouts in the attics or basements.

Several young men joined partisan groups in the forests. We heard rumors that Russian partisans had also become active in our vicinity. They were hounded by the Gestapo and the Ukrainian police, like wild animals. The partisans built underground bunkers in the forests, but when they tried to get food supplies in nearby villages, many were betrayed by the local peasants. We heard of fierce battles in which the poorly armed young boys and girls fought against overwhelming odds and inflicted casualties on the Gestapo before they perished. Peasants often came to the city and told of massacres in the forests.

The Germans did not waste anything; they collected the clothes of the victims, and ordered Jewish women to launder them in the public bathhouse. They had the first pick of the clothes and sent those to Germany, the rest were sold in the local stores. One day a friend of our family, engineer Platt, came into our house sobbing: he had just recognized on the street the dress his wife wore on the day she had been taken away.

We felt doomed, abandoned, and the world was silent...

We did not know then that the method of mass murder by shooting, which had been practiced by the "Sonderkommandos" in our area, might be superseded by more refined methods. On October 25, 1941, Adolf Eichmann, approved a proposal to use mobile gas vans to kill Jews. Dr. Brack, of euthanasia fame, was willing to help provide his own chemists and designs for building those infernal machines. One of their concerns was to prevent exposing their own soldiers from witnessing the terrible atrocities committed against defenseless civilians.

These mass murderers did not come from some remote jungles; they came from the heart of Christian Europe, from one of Europe's most advanced and "civilized" nation! In his book "Ordinary People", Christopher Browning follows one of these Sonderkommandos, the Reserve Police Battalion 101, which had operated in our area. They originated in Hamburg, and were made up of "ordinary men", dockworkers, policemen, lawyers, shopkeepers, teachers and others. Within a few weeks they turned into mass murderers of innocent men, women and children. A myth developed in Germany after the war, that those men who refused to shoot innocent people were executed. Christopher Browning reveals the fact that these men were given a choice! Those who refused to shoot innocent people were simply excused from that assignment and none paid with his life. Few, however, asked to be excused!

One winter morning, I walked out on the porch. The yard was covered with freshly fallen snow and the tree branches were bending under the weight of icicles that glistened like crystals in the sun. I felt so overwhelmed by the beauty of nature but my heart contracted with pain at the thought of our impending doom. Perhaps, this was the last time that, in my innocence, I asked God "why?"

The hiding place that my father built was in the attic of grandmother's house. He made a false wall, disguised as a bookshelf, not unlike the one I saw a few years ago in Amsterdam, where Anne Frank's family was hidden. We went to sleep only partially undressed and before dawn, when the "akcias" usually began, we made our way to the attic.

I remember how my father carried me, half asleep, to the shelter. We had stored there blankets and pillows as well as water and dried bread. At daybreak, if the Gestapo did not arrive in town, we went down. Mother prepared a warm meal, and another day in the ghetto began.

I look back today in disbelief how we placed our hope for survival in such a flimsy hiding place. Every SS-man and Ukrainian Policeman must have smashed many of these fake "bookcases" in their searches for Jews!

News of killings and atrocities in many communities around us also reached our town and we feared more "akcias" were in store. The Germans always tried to calm the population; they said that if everybody worked hard and handed over what was demanded of them to the authorities there would be no more killings.

The German commandant of the city told the Judenrat that if the Jews gave him five kilograms of gold and other valuables, he would see to it that our town would be spared. The people in town collected the gold and gave it to him, hoping to save our town, but it was just another futile attempt.

A special order was issued for Jews to turn over their gold wedding bands that had previously been exempted. Mr. Doppler suggested to the Judenrat that fifty gold rings should be turned over to him personally. He had an immense greed for gold.

Years later, I heard people talk about the decency of the post war German government in paying large sums of money to Holocaust survivors. They paid only a small fraction of what their countrymen had robbed and they could never repay for the lost and shattered lives.

On the first day of Passover 1942, I found my mother in the kitchen crying silently. I had rarely seen her cry before and asked her what had happened. She told me between sobs that the Germans had burned the ghetto in a nearby town, and when the people tried to jump out of the burning buildings they were all shot. Thus, our hiding place in the attic was totally useless.

The expectation that the gold that was collected would spare our town proved to be a false hope and during the Passover of 1942 the second "akcia" took place in Horodenka.

When the news reached us a few days before, that the Gestapo and their helpers were heading for our town, many people tried to hide wherever they could. Some built elaborate underground bunkers; others tried to hide with a friendly Christian family. My father took our family again to the flourmill where he worked. The day before we left, I said goodbye to my dearest childhood friend, Genia Reis. We met near the exit of the ghetto; she and her family were going to hide in an abandoned brick factory and I was certain that I shall see her again in a few days.

The "akcia" started at dawn with the usual shouts of "Juden Raus" (Jews out) resounding throughout the ghetto as the Gestapo and their helpers swept with their dogs and searched in every nook and cranny for terrified and defenseless people.

In the early morning of the second day I was awakened in our hiding place by the plaintive whistle of a locomotive. I found out later that on that train bound for the Belzec death camp was my childhood friend Genia Reis. Genia had brown eyes and lovely brown curls. She loved comic books and always insisted that some day she would live with her aunt in America and become a famous singer. I could never match her exciting dreams for the future, she always excelled. Genia was only thirteen years old.

On the third day, when the shooting and shouting stopped, we made our way to the ghetto, fearful of what we shall find there, or rather finding out who was no longer with us. Pitiful crying and wailing came from every house we passed. As we entered Grandmother's house, a weeping aunt Zlata threw her arms around me and held me tight. She had lost her only child, my oldest cousin Wisia, nineteen. All the cousins had looked up to her. She was a pretty girl of small build, with dark curly hair. She had finished the gymnasium (high school) and was a very gifted dress designer. I watched with admiration as she made lovely flowers out of velvet and different scraps of material for the cotillion ball at the gymnasium. She also liked to comb my long hair and arranged it like a crown on my head.

My poor aunt was desperate. She told us that someone had brought her a note that had been thrown out of the train. Our teacher of Jewish religion in the public school wrote that she was together with Wisia and would take care of her. We were all grief-stricken and I felt guilty. Why did I survive and not Wisia? She was an only child; she was all that my aunt had.

As happened after the first "akcia", the Germans reassured the remaining Jews, especially those who worked in different essential jobs, that they would be allowed to live and some people believed it. We did not know then, that on January 20, 1942, in the Berlin suburb of Wannsee, the Nazi leadership had drawn up plans for the annihilation of all European Jews. "The Final Solution", the euphemism for murder on a scale never seen before, had already been set in motion.

The news trickled through to us about the death camps of Belzec and Treblinka and about the gas vans of Chelmno. Hopelessness and desperation demoralized some people. Some turned to religion saying "surely the Messiah will come now at this time of our greatest need". They drew scorn from others who questioned the absence of God in the death camps. There were even those who became superstitious, using cards to predict the end of the horror. Still, most people suffered in quiet desperation.

The third "akcia" started in September 1942. Once again, the Gestapo and their helpers spread through the ghetto searching for Jews. The horror and the atrocities are hard to describe. We heard stories of some resistance: one young man, I believe he was a barber's apprentice, hid behind the door with an ax and, when the Gestapo entered the house, he struck and killed one of them. He and his entire family were killed on the spot; they did not evade death but they were saved from the dreadful journey in cattle cars, which was the fate of all other Jews caught on that day. We also heard stories of terrible betrayal and anguish:

one Jewish policeman who did not find a sufficient number of people to bring to the assembly point, revealed the hiding place of his family, in order to save his own life. When this became known, he was shunned by most people but also pitied by others. That the Nazi thugs could bring a Jew to commit such a terrible act of betrayal shocked us to the core!

All Jews found in homes and bunkers were brought to the railroad station and packed into cattle cars for transportation to the Belzec death camp. The "akcia" continued for two days. Jews caught after the trains left, were shot at the Jewish cemetery of Horodenka.

My family and I survived this "akcia" by hiding again in the flourmill. After the killers left, we returned to the ghetto. My Uncle Nathan Rosenbaum and his son Max, 14, had been on the train bound for Belzec. Most of the inhabitants of the ghetto had been taken away and their homes were sealed. The Germans wanted to make sure that they got the first pick of the spoils, before the locals did the plundering.

Horodenka, where Jews had lived since the seventeenth century, was declared "Judenrein", free of Jews. Within a few days, only those who had a special "V" permit (valuable Jew) could remain in town. All remaining Jews were taken to the ghetto in Kolomyja. Horodenka had ceased to exist as a Jewish "shtetl".

We assembled for the last time at my grandmother's house. The situation was desperate. My father had a V-permit that allowed him to remain in town, but he could not keep mother, brother or me with him. He decided to send us to his sister in Zaleszczyki, where Jews did not yet live in a ghetto, hoping to bring us back as soon as he could find a secure hiding place for us.

My Uncle Jacob, his wife Gita and Dr. Zenezib, a dentist with whom my aunt worked, had found with the help of my uncle's Ukrainian "friend", Dr. Bialy, a hiding place with a Ukrainian peasant and they were preparing to leave. Years later, I found out that this very same peasant had murdered all three. Some people also related how Dr. Bialy was seen laughing and mocking some of the Jews who, after having been discovered, were paraded through town.

[A few years ago, I received a phone call from a woman in the Midwest who had read on the Internet a speech I had given at Emory University. She claimed that her father, Dr. Bialy, had saved many Jews and was recognized by "Yad Va'shem" (Holocaust Memorial in Jerusalem) as a Righteous Among The Nations. I tried to find out more about this from Yad Va'shem, but they did not seem to have any record of this.]

We were all very concerned about our grandmother who was weak and ill, and would not survive a trip to the next ghetto. The family decided to spare her further suffering and to put her to sleep with a lethal injection.

My Uncle Jacob was a chemist and the family decided that while she was taking her afternoon nap, he would give her the injection. Her children would bury her with honor and recite at her grave the traditional mourner's prayer – the Kaddish. In the afternoon, my parents, Aunt Zlata, cousin Bella, little Wisia, Julek and I sat in a room next to her bedroom. When my uncle entered her bedroom we all sat motionless, tears running down our faces. A few minutes later, the door opened and my uncle came out sobbing. He apologized to us, saying, that he could not do it. My poor uncle, not even his great love for his mother could turn him into a mercy killer. I don't know what others in the room felt, but for me it was such a deep sorrow, knowing what was awaiting her. But I also felt some relief, because I loved my "Babcia" so very much…

My uncle then gave each person in the room, including the children, a poison pill. We had to promise that we would use it only as a last resort.

During the next few days, a few people who had jumped from the trains bound for Belzec began to trickle back to town. My cousin Max was one of them and he described the horrible conditions on that train. Two hundred people were packed in each cattle car, with the men separated from the women. The heat was hellish, the thirst intolerable. Only a small window covered with barbed wire let some air in. Some of the people tore away the barbed wire with their bare hands and, as the train slowed down around the curves, they jumped. The Gestapo and the Ukrainian police were shooting at the people trying to escape. My cousin pleaded with his father to jump, but he refused, though he encouraged my cousin to try to save his life. Max told us that his father said: "it is nearer than farther", meaning the end is near now and he did not want to live any more.

My friend Genia's father, Mr. Reis, also returned but I shall never forget his desperate and battered face when he learned that his son Lusiek, who had jumped with him, did not make it back.

Zaleszczyki and Tluste

We heard that across the Dniester River the situation was somewhat better, Jews were not forced to live in ghettos. My father decided to send mother, Julek and me to Zaleszczyki. My father's "friend", a Pole named Franek, came with a horse and wagon to Horodenka to fetch us. During past visits to our house, Franek would seat me on his lap and recount how my father had saved his life during World War I. My father was an officer in the Austro-Hungarian army and Franek was his orderly. My father trusted him fully. The few valuables we still possessed were given to Franek for safekeeping.

We put on peasants' clothes and prepared for the trip. We said goodbye to my father in front of our old house. My father embraced me and, for the first and only time, I saw him cry. It scared and puzzled me: why was he crying? We were going to be back together soon, as he had promised. Wasn't he trying to find for us a good hiding place and bring us back to Horodenka? Alas, this was the last time I saw my father.

The fear of being detected by Germans or Ukrainians diminished any pleasure that this, our first trip outside the ghetto in many months, could have offered. Zaleszczyki was about 25 km from the former home of my father's family. We arrived in Zaleszczyki tired and sad because father stayed behind in Horodenka. Before I had time to see the city of my birth, we learned that the town had been declared "Judenrein", free of Jews. All Jews had to leave within twenty-four hours for the neighboring ghetto of Tluste.

The long sad procession of old and young started on a beautiful autumn day. The young people walked, the old and the sick made the journey on horse-drawn wagons. We walked leisurely, with police escorting us, but most knew that they would never see the town again.

In Tluste we found a chaotic situation. Thousands of people were crowded in a few narrow streets of the ghetto. The Judenrat assigned housing for everyone. We wound up in one room with four or five families, about twenty people. Each family huddled in a corner. My mother, my brother and I had a bunk, crudely made out of planks on which we all slept. The sanitary conditions were appalling. There was no running water and we had no soap and no way to keep clean. Food was scarce and our meager resources ran out very quickly, we had to depend on the "Kennkarte" (ID for food allotment) and the community soup kitchen. Our only hope was that our father would soon find a hiding place for us and bring us back to Horodenka.

My mother left Julek and me in the ghetto of Tluste and returned to Horodenka to see whether anything could be arranged for her mother, but she was caught up by the evacuation of the Jews from Horodenka to the Ghetto of Kolomyia and was forced to march there. With great difficulty she managed to return from there to the Ghetto in Tluste. She described to us how the few remaining Jews from Horodenka were driven on foot to Kolomyia. My grandmother and a few other old and sick people were put on horse-drawn wagons. The remainder had to run as Germans and Ukrainian police on horses were beating them with whips. My cousin Max who had been at the end of the long row of marchers was absorbing much of the beatings. She put her coat over his shoulders trying to protect him. The horror they found when they reached the Kolomyja ghetto was beyond imagination. There was no room for all the people in the ghetto. Starvation and sickness were taking daily a heavy toll. My mother finally found a local family who allowed my grandmother to sleep in the attic of the stable. For a long time I had visions of my poor grandmother climbing the ladder to the attic. I don't know how long she, aunt Zlata and cousin Max, who were with her, remained alive. In Kolomyja, as elsewhere, the "akcias" continued unabated. I always regretted that we were not able to spare my grandmother all that additional suffering, as we had intended.

Once a week, at an appointed time, my father called us. He usually spoke with my mother at a public phone. Use of public phones was strictly forbidden for Jews, but we had no choice. Mother told to us that father was almost ready to bring us back. One day in the fall of 1942, my mother was not feeling well and my brother and I went to talk with our father. We stood together in the public phone booth when, suddenly, I saw my brother turn pale like a ghost. All I heard him say was "when?" I did not need an explanation because I fully understood that my father was gone. The secretary at the flourmill told us that when the Gestapo came to take him away, his boss insisted that the books were not in order and that he still needed him. The Gestapo men then said that they would wait 24 hours, till he brought the books in order. My father completed the work and was taken away. I heard that the people who were rounded up on September 6, 1942, were brought to a large estate on the way to the railroad station. They were kept in a warehouse for two days without food or water, and marched, four abreast to the railroad station. A selection took place at the station; the young and strong were sent to the notorious Janowska camp, older men, women and the children were sent to Belzec. I have never been able to find out for certain, but I believe that my father also perished in Belzec.

When my mother heard the news she was totally devastated. We tried to comfort her, as best we could. She lay on the bunk and sobbed uncontrollably. We were now left on our own without any hope of ever escaping from this hellish place.

A typhus epidemic raged in the ghetto and my brother Julek also became ill. The people with whom we shared the room insisted that we take him away to a hospital because typhus is highly contagious. The community had taken over one house and called it a "hospital", though it had nothing even remotely resembling one. There were no doctors, nurses, nor medicine of any kind and there was very little food. Families stayed with their loved ones and tried to take care of them as best they could, but most patients died. My brother ran a very high fever and was delirious for several days. We made a makeshift stretcher out of an old door, placed him on it and carried him on that cold winter day to the "hospital". The one story little house was crowded with the sick and dying. The place was not heated. I bartered some clothes for a log of wood to heat the room in which my brother lay. I borrowed a saw and started cutting the log. My hands were numb from the freezing cold and I could barely hold the saw. I cried in my frustration but continued to struggle. Finally I managed to cut the log and ran with it to the "hospital". We placed the wood in the stove, but it would not burn; the peasant had sold me green wood. It only smoked and filled the little room with a choking smoke. We had to open the window and let the freezing cold come in.

The situation in Tluste worsened as people were being caught on the streets for forced labor. Everyone built a bunker in his home. The "hospital" had a bunker as well. It was a deep tunnel dug under the house that one entered through a hidden trap door. The opening to the bunker was under a metal plate next to the stove placed there to store kindling wood and catch falling sparks or ashes. One day, when we heard that the Ukrainian police had just entered the ghetto, everyone jumped into the bunker, including my mother and I. Someone pulled a bed with a corpse of an old woman over the entrance to the bunker. As we sat there, I pictured the Ukrainians shooting my brother as he lay defenseless and alone. I could not bear the thought of it, and jumped out of the bunker. As the police entered the house, I took off my coat and when they asked what I was doing there, I said that I was a nurse. They looked around and left. Apparently this time they were looking for able-bodied men for forced labor. This was not a "shooting party" of the old and sick, as had happened so many times before. My mother also tried to get out, but some people held her back, she was quite upset with me, yet I think she understood that I could not do otherwise.

Before my father was taken away, he sent to us our cousins Bella, 17 and Wisia, 9, who had been left all alone. Bella had long brown braids and was a very kind and serious young girl. She took care of her nine year old sister Wisia (there were two Wisias in our family). Little Wisia was a deaf-mute child and Bella could best communicate with her. Wisia probably never heard the shot that ended her short life only a few months later.

My father's cousin, Jonah Schechter, who lived in Tluste was a very kind man. When he heard about our living conditions, he found for us a little room not far from his house. My mother now had to care for four children. Our funds and belongings one could barter for food, like clothing or other valuables, were running out quickly. The rations we received were very small and we were constantly hungry, especially my brother who was recovering from typhus. I had never known how painful hunger could be, it seemed that every cell in our bodies cried out for nourishment. My mother became extremely thin, always trying to give what little food there was to the children. At first, the hunger kept us awake at night, but as time went on, we became more and more listless and apathetic.

Jonah Schechter asked me if I wanted to earn some money by selling notions to the peasants on market days. I jumped at the opportunity of peddling some of the merchandise he had saved from his store. I had to take off my armband with the Star of David, get out of the ghetto and mingle with the crowds of Poles and Ukrainians who came to town on market day. My blond hair and so called "non-Semitic" features helped and I sold needles, threads and all kinds of notions. I had to keep a keen eye at all times for the police, because leaving the ghetto or walking without the armband was punishable by death. In this way, I earned a bit of money and could buy with it some grain. Jonah had hidden under the floorboard of his kitchen two grind-stones, the ownership of which was strictly forbidden under the threat of death. At night, we gathered in his house, stationed a lookout for the police, and ground the wheat into flour.

Mother mixed the flour with water for a soup, or she baked flat cakes on top of the stove; when she had a few potatoes to add to the soup it was a real treat. We would also roast the potato peels on the stove. The crispy potato peels with a bit of salt tasted quite good and helped to lessen the gnawing hunger that never left us. I can only imagine now how terrible it must have been for my mother to watch her children and nieces starve and not be able to help. She always tried secretly to give the children a bit more of her meager portion, but she lost a lot of weight and became quite listless.

Life was very difficult and brutal during that winter. My older cousin Bella and I tried to do most of the chores that required being outside of the house, because we feared that my brother might be caught for forced labor. We had to carry water from the only water pump in the ghetto, over a mile away. On cold days, my fingers would stick to the handle of the metal bucket. We did not have warm clothes, since we had left home before the winter began. When we left home, mother had urged me to put on my best clothes, so I put on layers of dresses and blouses, as many as I could, including my only velvet party dress! One day, as I went out to get water, I suddenly saw before me the chief of the Ukrainian police with his helpers. He stopped me, asked where I was going and whether I knew that when he walked through the ghetto he did not want to see any filthy Jews. He slapped me in the face and told me to run. As I ran up the hill, I heard shots being fired but they missed me. I came home without water but did not tell my mother what had happened, not wanting to worry her even more. But she did find out because some concerned neighbors ran into the house after me to see if I was O.K. I was more careful in the future, so as not to run into that brutal beast as he walked through the streets of the ghetto.

In the ghetto of Tluste also lived my aunt, Netti Rosenbaum, my father's sister, with her daughter Lusia. When the Russians withdrew, they took my uncle Dr. Michael Rosenbaum, a medical doctor, with them, even though he was over forty five years old and past the recruiting age for the army but they said that they needed medical doctors during the war.

One day when my mother and I were visiting with my aunt Netti and cousin Lusia, we met there a Russian man who earlier had rescued my younger cousin, Julia, by taking her with him to his home in the Ukraine. He brought greetings from her and a letter in which she wrote that she was all right and that this man could be trusted. We were especially relieved to see a prearranged marker on the letter, which meant that she was writing without coercion, and that everything she wrote was true.

We looked at this man as a saving angel. At least one of our own had a chance to escape certain death. My mother sighed and said how happy she would be if there were someone who would be willing to take her daughter. He looked at me for a moment and said: get her ready, in two days I shall take her to a far-away village to a friend of mine and tell him that she is my cousin; I shall also get for her Aryan papers. My mother was overjoyed, she ran home quickly to tell the good news to my brother and my cousins. Everyone felt so happy for me.

The next two days were quite hectic. Mother borrowed a little suitcase for me, she patched up my clothes and repaired my shoes to make me look more presentable. She spent hours trying to teach me the catechism and how to behave in church. Having been a teacher in Polish public schools before the war, she had to be present in class when the priest came to instruct the children, so she was quite familiar with Christian rituals. As time passed, my resolve to leave weakened. I knew that I would never see mother, my brother or my cousins again. Mother kept repeating over and over again: SOMEONE MUST SURVIVE TO TELL THE WORLD. She was convinced that if the world knew what was happening to us, the great powers would intervene and not allow for this horror to continue. She did not know that the world, or at least the top Allied officials in London and Washington had been informed in great detail about the conditions in the ghettos and in the extermination camps by, among others, Jan Karski, a courrier of the Polish underground.

[Over half a century later, I listened to Mr. Karski relate his war-time experiences. In November 1942, Mr. Karski was smuggled into the Warsaw ghetto and into the extermination camp at Belzec. He saw the starving people, the piles of dead corpses stacked like cordwood, and the hellish conditions of these places. He took pictures and listened to testimonies. He was also smuggled into the inferno of Auschwitz, dressed as a Ukrainian policeman. After he made his way to London and Washington, he described in detail to British and American leaders what he had seen and heard. His reports were met with skepticism. For instance, Felix Frankfurter, a Jew and Associate Justice of the Supreme Court, listened with disbelief and told Karski that "I remember every word you said, Mr. Karski, but a man like me talking to a man like you must be frank. So I say, I am unable to believe what you told me." President Roosevelt did not allow this information to be passed on to American Jewish leaders. He is reported to have said that he did not want Hitler to use this information as propaganda to support his claim that the Allies had gone to war because of the Jews.]

The crematoria were going full steam and the world was silent...

One of our greatest fears was that we would all be killed and no one would know our fate. The Germans told us that even if one of us survives and tries to tell the world what happened here, no one would believe him.

In the evening of the second day, I was supposed to steal my way out of the ghetto, take off my armband, go to the railroad station, buy a ticket, get on the train and take a seat in a designated compartment where the Russian man would wait for me. Of course, every step of the way was fraught with great danger.

As the time approached to leave, I said goodbye to my brother and cousins and walked with my mother to the border of the ghetto. It was a dark and freezing night and we were shivering as we walked through the crammed and filthy streets. I tried to chisel into my memory the horror pictures around me: starving and sick people lying on door steps and emaciated children huddling in doorways. I told myself that I must remember everything. As we approached the fence around the ghetto, I took off my armband with the Star of David and embraced my mother. We stood like this for a while, without saying a word. It became very clear to me that this would be a final goodbye, that I shall never see her or my brother again. I imagined that no Jews would survive the war and that I might be the only one left, living alone among strangers and forced to live with a lie. I could never accept the Christian faith, a faith which spoke of love and compassion yet counted among its faithfuls so many murderers. In my youthful mind I thought that either the teaching was wrong or they have not learned anything in two thousand years. I did not want to live with and among killers; I did not want to live among people who, actively or passively, had participated in the destruction of the Jews. It was too high a price to pay, even if this were my only hope to survive. I did not want to live in the world where my people were so brutally murdered, in a country where the earth was soaked with Jewish blood. At that moment, I preferred to go down with my people.

I told my mother that I decided not to leave and she did not say a word. She held my hand tightly. I put my armband back and we walked in silence to our room. She did not urge me to change my mind; she understood that the decision had to be mine, even though I was only fourteen years old.

My brother and my cousins were stunned to see me back; I had a chance to get out of this hell but did not take it. I would like to believe that they were also glad that I returned and that I did not abandon them. I shall always be grateful to my mother that she let me make that important decision; it gave me a few more weeks together with her, my brother and my cousins.

My mother made one more attempt to save my life. She would have also gone to any length to save my brother but this was much more difficult, since it was easier to identify Jewish men. In the town of Tluste lived one of her former Polish colleagues, a teacher and his family. We made our way to his house. She knocked on the door; he opened the door a crack but would not let us in. Mother begged him to help me, repeating that I did not look Jewish, that nobody would recognize me in this strange town and that I could serve as a maid in his house, but to no avail. She then begged him to give me his daughter's birth certificate or her baptismal papers, which could save my life. He refused and slammed the door in my mother's face.

She seemed so desperate in her attempt to save at least one of her children. I felt so sorry for her and tried to tell her to please stop since I did not want to leave anyhow. Today, I am a mother and a grandmother, but I cannot fathom what a terrible anguish it must have been for my poor mother to be forced to choose just one of her children for possible survival.

During the bitter winter of 1942, all five of us lived in one small room. Two beds occupied the length of the room head to toe; a small wood-burning hearth was in one corner, and a little table in another. Above the hearth, a square hole in the wall, was an opening to the next apartment, through which we used to communicate with our neighbors. If there were disturbances in the ghetto, they would knock on the wooden door to warn us. News and rumors spread quickly through the ghetto. No matter how terrible the stories were, we soon learned not to doubt; the realities were worse than anyone could have imagined.

We spent most of the days trying to gather some food, which consisted of going to the Judenrat for the rations or bartering a piece of clothing, or anything of value, as long we still had some. We hunted for a piece of wood to keep from freezing in Poland's bitter cold winters. Sometimes we found a piece of wood from a broken fence or a bombed out house. The destroyed synagogue on the corner was stripped of all wood; it was painful to see this house of prayer so desolate. Day by day, it became more and more difficult to sustain bare life. We huddled on the beds to keep warm and talked about the loved ones we lost, about the incomprehensible cruelty of our oppressors, and the sadness we felt by the total abandonment on the part of the civilized world. Occasionally, we recalled the happy days before the war, but as time went on we did it less often, it was much too painful... Mother still prayed sometimes, or rather cried out to God, in Yiddish "Gotenu hob rachmunes of di kinder" (Dear God have pity on the children) but God was also silent...

Those long fitful nights filled with nightmares and the days of agony, hunger and fear seemed to blend together. One day followed the other, no holidays, no Sabbath to distinguish one day from another. It is precisely the holidays and Sabbath that we feared the most, since the roundups and killings took place most often on those days. The markers on our calendar were the dates of the "akcias"!

The Nazi thugs denied legitimacy to Sigmund Freud's teachings and to psychology in general, but they did not shy away from using every psychological device to try to break the spirit of our people. We were most vulnerable on the days, which in times past, marked our holidays and celebrations but had now become days of agony for us.

Eventually, my mother contracted typhus. She was already very weakened from starvation. Our doctors were not allowed to practice, no medicines were available in the ghetto and we could not get any help for her. We tried our best to take care of her. One evening, I felt very hot and it became obvious that I had also come down with typhus. I lay down next to her in bed. Suddenly, there was a knock from our next-door neighbor. We had an arranged communication system from one house to the other in case of danger. The neighbor told us that the Ukrainian police and the Germans had just entered the ghetto and she urged us to hide. We had no hiding place in that house, we felt trapped and helpless. My mother sat up in bed, turned on the light, and fell back on the pillow. I started to cry. She embraced me, and spoke to me in Yiddish, which she had never done before, saying "di werst noch gliklich sain main kind" loosely translated "you will still be happy one day, my child". Though I was running a high fever and was intermittently delirious, I still remember wondering what a strange thing to say under those circumstances! Those were her last words, her poor heart gave out... She was only thirty-nine years old.

What happened during the next few hours is not very clear to me. I was shivering from the very high fever and was unconscious most of the time. I recall that later that night, my brother knelt next to my bed and told me that our mother had died. I tried to look down where my mother lay on the floor covered with a white sheet, but it was difficult for me to turn my head and focus my eyes. The flame of the candle at her side danced before my eyes, and then all went dark for a very long time.

Weeks later, my brother told me some of the details of that horrible night. He said, that some kind neighbors gave him a clean white sheet to wrap my mother's body, he and my cousins put her gently on the floor, as is our custom, lit a memorial candle and said Kadish (the mourner's prayer) for her. He then borrowed a wheelbarrow from a neighbor and under cover of darkness brought my mother to the Jewish cemetery of Tluste where he buried her. He told me that he put a bottle with her name in the grave and he promised that one day we would erect a gravestone.

[Half a century later, I returned to the cemetery in Tluste. I knew that my mother was buried there and that I probably stood just a few feet from her grave, but there was no way for me to locate it. An impressive memorial had been erected over the many unmarked graves a few years ago by survivors living in Israel. I scooped up some soil and later buried it in our family plot in Atlanta, Georgia.]

The epidemic of typhus was at its peak and twenty to thirty people died each day. We tried to bury our dead secretly, to hide from the Germans the extent of the epidemic that was raging in the ghetto. Jews unable for work were the first ones to be murdered. It was rumored that the epidemic had started after seventy Jews who had been imprisoned in Buczacz were released and sent back to Tluste. Most of them came down with typhus. The sanitary conditions in the ghetto were appalling. It was impossible to control the infestation with lice, the carriers of typhus. Those insects added additional suffering and misery to our tormented nights.

I don't remember very much of the days and weeks that followed, since I was unconscious and delirious most of the time. My brother told me later that once he managed to get a Jewish doctor to come clandestinely and examine me. The doctor found that I had double pneumonia as well as typhus and he gave Julek little hope for my recovery.

My brother attributed my survival to the "miracle of the eggs". Next to the ghetto lived a Polish man who had once worked with my father in the eggs export business. He found out about us four orphaned children and he came to visit us, always bringing along some eggs. We had no other food, but these eggs kept us alive that winter. This man not only enabled us to survive, but he brought to that world of darkness and despair a ray of hope, of decency, and of compassion. To my great regret, I do not remember his name.

When spring arrived, my brother and cousins took me outside to sit in the sun. I was very weak and could not walk unassisted. I wanted to go to the cemetery where my mother was buried and my brother promised to take me there when I got better. With my recovery came a terrible hunger.

One day, my brother sold some of my mother's clothes and with the money he got, we went to a clandestine bakery to buy a piece of bread. We got half a loaf of freshly baked bread; it smelled so wonderful and we were so hungry. We took a little piece, and then a little more, and before long, the bread was gone. We were full of remorse and shame because we had nothing left to bring to our hungry cousins. We both cried in shame and frustration that hunger had brought us down to such a state! It never happened again, but the memory of it still haunts me.

In May, the news spread through the ghetto that the Gestapo in the neighboring town of Buczacz was preparing to come to Tluste and that an "akcia" was imminent. The ghetto became deserted, some people fled to the fields and forests, others hid in elaborate bunkers. My brother and I went to the Judenrat to find out what was happening. One man from the Judenrat saw us and asked: what are you children doing here, don't you know that the Gestapo is on the way? We told him that we had no hiding place; he quickly wrote out work cards for us, and instructed us to go to the camp in Lisovce, hoping that the Gestapo might not get there.

Labor Camp Lisowce

The Germans had established in the vicinity of the town of Tluste six large agricultural farms where they used Jewish slave laborers, as well as peasants from surrounding villages, as workers.

The manager of the six agricultural estates (folwarks) in that area was a German by the name of Paul Friedrich Fati who was rumored to be a decent man. It was said that if you worked for Fati, you would be treated decently and be protected from the Gestapo. You had to have an "Arbeitskarte" (work card) to be assigned to one of the six estates: Kozia Gora, Szarszenuwka, Holobczynce, Rorzyzuwka, Szypowce and Lisowce.

We started walking out of the town. On the way, we saw entire families running with their children. We saw Ukrainian thugs robbing and beating people as they tried to flee. Some local peasants ran with their sacks slung over their shoulders towards the ghetto, ready to loot and rob the defenseless Jews. By evening, we arrived in the camp of Lisowce. The place was deserted. Most of the workers had fled, fearing that the Gestapo would try to round them up as well. We found an empty barrack, huddled in a corner, and fell asleep. Next day, many of the workers returned, since it seemed to be a quiet day. We met the Jewish leader of the camp, who assigned us to a barrack and in the morning we went to work with an assigned crew. We worked in the fields, hoeing sugar beets, corn, potatoes, tobacco and "koksagyz" plants. Kok-saghyz looked like tobacco and was supposed to produce a rubber like latex. The Russians had introduced this plant to the region and the Germans continued farming it, in hopes of producing rubber for their war machine. When the leaves were picked, a white liquid started to drip from the stock. Working in the hot sun while tending to these plants gave us headaches. I never found out whether the Germans managed to produce any rubber from these plants. We worked from early morning till late in the day. At midday, they brought us some soup and water. We also got soup in the evening after work and some bread.

After the starvation diet in the ghetto, soup and some bread was a great improvement and in the open field one could also find some carrots, sweet sugar beets and other vegetables to add to our diet.

The second day after our arrival at the camp, the news reached us from the ghetto of Tluste that an "akcia" was in progress there. After the "akcia" was over, I decided to go to Tluste to see if our cousins and my aunt Netti and her daughter Lusia were safe. They had been hiding in what everyone thought was one of the safest bunkers in town.

As I approached the town, I had to pass the Jewish cemetery. The sight was unbelievable: bloody and torn clothes were strewn everywhere. Torn dollar bills and local currency, which the victims preferred to destroy rather than leave to the murderers, were lying around. Near the entrance of the cemetery, was a huge freshly dug grave barely covered with soil. The peasants were afraid to pass near it, saying that the earth moved over the grave and that blood oozed from it like a fountain. I walked to the ghetto where corpses were still lying around. The door to our room was ajar. The room had been ransacked and no one was there. My cousin Bella 17, and her deaf-mute sister Wisia, 9, had been killed. I proceeded to look for my Aunt Netti and cousin Lusia, only to find out that the "foolproof" bunker in which they were hiding had been discovered and all the people were shot.

I returned to the Lisowce camp with the sad news. Of our once large family, only Julek and I now remained. Most of the people in the camp had lost loved ones. Sadness and despair gripped us all.

Reports of killings in the neighboring work camps made us realize that the camps were also not safe. A group of young Jews made contact with a Polish underground partisan group and arranged to meet with them in a nearby forest. I stood to the side as my brother and the other older boys were having discussions with them. It developed that they did not want to accept any of our people into their group, unless we had weapons or money with which to buy guns. When they found out that we had neither, they left. We were very disappointed, but we did not know whether there really was a chance to join a fighting group or whether it was a ploy to get money from us.

In the neighboring camp of Rorzanowka, one of the Polish supervisors – I think his name was Zawacki – had known my father. Julek and I went to see him and asked whether he could help us get away on Aryan papers. He said that he was willing to help me but could not do anything for my brother, since Jewish boys could be easily identified. I thanked him and told him that I would not leave without my brother.

In Lisowce, some of us worked in the stables, some worked in the blacksmith shop, the majority worked in the fields. Very early in the morning, the Ukrainian guard would assign work to us. We would march to the fields together with some of the local peasants who were also conscripted to work for the Germans but they were free to go home after work and were probably paid for their labor. I can still recall the columns of workers marching with hoes over their shoulders. The peasants would usually break out in a song. When we crossed the bridge we would see the mist rising over the river and an observer could imagine an idyllic summer scene of happy farmers going to work in their fields. Alas, those fields were soon to become killing grounds soaked with the blood of the innocents.

We also worked often at the threshing machine. One day in July, the camp was full of rumors of an impending "akcia". A lot of people fled to the woods and fields, and my brother and I also ran away. We lay in a wheat field in the hot July sun for many hours. We were terribly thirsty but were afraid to move. The day passed quietly, and we returned to the camp. That night, my brother worked the night shift at the threshing machine and my group was to start later. I went to a Ukrainian woman who lived close to the field and asked her for some food to bring to my brother. She was a poor peasant woman who lived in a one-room little shack working for food and wages in the fields of more prosperous farmers. She had a good heart and, on occasions, she shared some food with me. That evening, as she was cooking a potato soup, I kept asking her if it was done, since I was very nervous and anxious to bring some food to my brother, but she kept delaying me. Finally, she gave me a pot of soup and I ran with it to the field, where my brother worked. We sat together and ate.

I lay down to sleep next to a haystack, because I was to start my shift in the morning. Next to me lay a woman with two children, a boy of about four and a girl of six. Children were not allowed in the camp, but the mother was hiding them. Before dawn, shots awakened us. When I opened my eyes I saw two Ukrainian policemen and an SS-man standing over us. One shot was fired and the little girl was hit in the foot. She bled profusely and whimpered quietly. We were told to stand up, raise our hands and walk to an assigned place. When we got there, a group of people was already sitting on the ground with their hands behind their backs. Men were ordered to dig graves and the shooting continued. I was relieved that I did not see my brother among the doomed and hoped that he had escaped.

I never saw a more beautiful sunrise. I felt very calm and reasoned that, if our sages and teachers were right and there is a world beyond (Olam Ha'bah), then all would be well and I shall soon be reunited with my parents, family, and friends. But if there were only this world of horror, then to be finished with all this suffering, humiliation, constant fear and hunger would also be a relief. I only hoped that they would shoot straight and it won't hurt too much. We said goodbye to each other. Nobody cried. No one pleaded for his life.

Suddenly, the German commandant of the camp came riding on a horse. We heard him scream at the Gestapo, that he needed us to complete the harvest and that they must stop the slaughter. The shooting stopped. Everyone scattered and ran into the fields and forests nearby, since we were afraid that the Gestapo might decide to continue the shooting. I called my brother's name as I ran, but no one responded. After a while I went back to the barracks and waited for him to return. A few people started to come back from hiding. At one point a young boy turned the corner and thinking it was Julek I ran to meet him, but I was mistaken.

We began to collect our fallen comrades scattered in the fields and in the barracks. Seventeen young boys and girls had been murdered on that day. Among them was my brother Julek, not quite eighteen years old.

In the evening I returned to the nearly deserted camp; most people had fled, fearing that the murderers would come back. I did not care any more; I lay in the barracks and cried. The following day, some of our people were told to dig up the temporary graves and move our dead to a mass grave. As they started digging, I saw my brother's clothes. I fainted and was carried back to the camp. I am sure that if I still had the poison pill that my uncle had given us, I would have gladly taken it.

A few days later, as we worked in a field near the river, one of my friends pointed out to me the new grave. I walked over and stood there for a moment. The Ukrainian guard screamed at me to return to work and then proceeded to urinate on the grave.

During the days that followed I was in a haze. I stopped going to work and wandered aimlessly around. One day, as I walked with my head down, I saw before me a pair of black boots. As I lifted my head, I saw our German camp commandant and I was sure that the end I had longed for had arrived. He asked my name and age. I lied and said that I was eighteen. Rather than being punished for not being at work, he told me to go to his villa and tell the cook to give me some food and clean clothes. I was stunned because I did not know then that, in spite of the fact that he was a cousin of Hans Frank, the notoriously vicious Gauleiter of Poland, he was a decent man. His Jewish cook Erna gave me some food to eat, my first meal in days. For the first time in many months I could wash up and put on clean clothes. One of the hard things to bear in camp was the total lack of sanitation. Our fitful sleep was not only interrupted by nightmares, but also made unbearable by lice. We wore the same clothes day in and day out and we also slept in them.

During that summer of 1943, I worked in the attic of the German commandant's villa, knitting sweaters that he sent to Germany. There I met a girl my age, we were both fifteen years old, who had also been left all alone. Being together with Fritzka helped me to find my bearings again and recover somewhat after the devastating blow of losing my brother. As we sat knitting, we talked about the families we had lost, about our life before the war, and even dreamed of a world after the war. We pledged to each other never to part, should we survive. The news was beginning to reach us about the uprising in the Warsaw ghetto and we envied those people who died fighting. A new will to go on was revived in us, a will to survive and to bear witness and, yes, to take revenge for all the innocent blood spilled. A desire to see this evil empire destroyed became stronger than ever.

News also began to trickle in about the German defeat at Stalingrad, and we thought that the German military fortune had been reversed. We heard rumors that large military transport trains with wounded German soldiers had been seen passing daily. Some people who worked for the Germans heard reports on the radio that many cities were abandoned by the Germans in the East, in what was called a "strategic withdrawal". Hope again began to stir in us.

One day, I met Mr. Zawacki and he told me that he was willing, now that Julek was gone, to help me get away on Aryan papers. I told him that it was too late, and that I preferred to live and die with my people.

I did attempt though to see Franek, my father's "friend". I longed to see a friendly face, someone who had known my family, and tell him of my sorrow. I exchanged my clothes and shoes for a peasant's outfit and started walking some 10 km to Franek's village. I walked barefoot, as was the custom among the peasants in our region. As I approached the police station in Tluste, I noticed a roadblock. I had no papers, but it was too late to turn back. When my turn came, I was asked for my papers. I spoke Ukrainian pretty well at that time, and I told them that I had come from the mountains to earn some money during the harvest and I did not know that I needed papers. Somehow, I must have been convincing enough because they let me go.

As I walked by the road and saw peasants peacefully tending their fields, I felt such a pain in my heart: why were we hounded like wild beasts? When I passed peasants on the road, I greeted them with the traditional greeting of "Blessed be Jesus Christ" and they answered, "May He be blessed for ever and ever". I wondered how they could accept Jesus as their savior and still be filled with so much hate? How could two thousand years of teaching a religion of "love" produce killers in such great numbers? These atrocities were not committed by some remote aboriginal tribe, it happened in the heart of Christian Europe!

By the time I got to Franek's house, it was already evening. I knocked on the door, Franek opened, but when he saw me, his first words were: "What are you doing here? They killed four Jews in the village, yesterday, you can't stay here". In my fantasy, I had imagined that he would embrace me, and that we would shed tears together at the fate of my family. It was a severe blow, but I recovered quickly. I told him that I did not want to endanger his family, that I would only like to stay overnight and leave early in the morning. I asked him if he could give me some food and a pair of old shoes. My feet were bleeding since I was not used to walking barefoot for so many miles. Franek told me that he did not have any shoes for me, I asked him if he had a pair of old rain boots that he could spare and he said that he did not. This was the man whom my father had trusted! The man who used to hold me on his knees and tell me how my father had saved his life. Buried in his garden were my uncle's medical instruments and other valuables. Franek allowed me to stay overnight in his barn and later at night brought me some food. I could hardly eat it, in spite of my great hunger.

Later that night, Franek came back with another man whom he introduced as a friend of my father's. He said that this man, whose name I don't remember, was willing to help me. The man said all the right things, how he was going to get false papers for me and help me get away to a large city, but something in the tone of his voice and his demeanor did not seem right. I was only fifteen, but I sensed danger. I had a feeling that he might call the police the next day to get the pound of sugar promised as a reward for bringing in a Jewish person. I thanked him and tried to sleep, but sleep did not come easy, even though I was exhausted. Franek's total lack of compassion and betrayal of trust hurt me deeply. Very early the next morning, when he came into the stable to milk the cows, I told him that I was leaving. He gave me half a loaf of bread but nothing to bind my bleeding feet. I left, sick at heart.

I did not fault him for being afraid to harbor a Jew, but what shocked and hurt me deeply was his total lack of empathy and compassion.

[After the war, when my cousin Julia came back to Zaleszczyki, she went to Franek and asked him to return her father's medical instruments and other valuables that he had hidden. He claimed that he did not have anything, that the Germans had taken everything away. She did not believe him and returned with the Soviet police who dug up his garden, retrieved everything and arrested him.]

My only desire, after the encounter with Franek, was to reach the camp, to be again with my people. I did not want to die like a dog by the wayside. If I had to die, the last thing I wanted to see, were Jewish eyes. I made my way back, stopping every few miles at the wayside shrines, crossing myself, imitating the local peasants in their adoration of the statues of the Virgin Mary. She was adorned in blue and gold robes and the flower offerings were wilting in the hot sun. I felt silly doing this and felt repelled by what seemed to me to be idolatry.

I made it back to the camp safely and was happy to be again with my friend Fritzka. We were usually assigned to the same work detail, we slept in the same bunk and shared every scrap of food.

One Sunday when we were not working, I decided to wash my hair. I melted some snow and was heating the water, when I heard a friend run by and scream that the Ukrainian police had been seen entering the camp. Only half dressed, I ran toward the stables where one could usually find a hiding place. Suddenly I felt someone put a heavy sheepskin coat over my shoulders and lead me away from the camp. It was a Ukrainian man from a nearby village who used to come to the camp and barter food with people who still had some things of value. I was not one of them since I no longer had anything but I used to see him around. He led me to a peasant's house near our compound and hid me under the straw in the attic. This time the police did not stop in our camp and drove on. When the news spread, that this Ukrainian peasant had endangered his own life to save a Jewish girl, he became a trusted hero among our people. He used to come often and even honored me with a proposal of marriage, disregarding the danger this would have entailed for him. Needless to say it was not something I considered for even a moment, but I thanked him anyway.

Sometime in the fall, we heard that a group of young Jews had formed a resistance group in the forests and that they were armed. One of them came to our camp for his sister. I met with him and he was willing to take me along. We arranged to meet in the next village, at an appointed time. Next day, I started walking along the river toward that village. I wore the only clothes I had, an old peasant's skirt and blouse. Suddenly I saw on the other side of the river two Ukrainian policemen on bicycles and felt a bit uneasy, but I continued to walk. The place near the well where we were to meet was deserted. I reasoned that having spotted the police they had fled. I was devastated. More than anything I wished for at that time, was that I had a gun, to make the murderers pay. A few days later, we heard that the police had hounded down the entire group of Jews and no one survived. Two Ukrainian policemen and a German were also killed.

On my way back to the camp, I saw two Jewish girls sitting on the side of the road and crying. They told me that some peasants from the village had raped them. I was, obviously, very upset. But on what scale does one measure this crime with death all around us?

The winter of 1943 was very severe. We worked outdoors, without gloves or stockings. Since I had bartered away my shoes for a Ukrainian outfit, I was walking around barefoot, even in the snow, until one of my friends made for me a pair of wooden shoes. When I tried to take these shoes off at night, I had to tear off the bloody rags from my feet. Lack of proper nutrition caused many carbuncles to form on my feet and my arms.

On some evenings after work, we assembled in the stables. It was a warm place and we sat around on the straw and talked. Occasionally, someone would start a song, a milk bucket serving as a drum. These were rare evenings, when most of the work was indoors and we were not as exhausted and frozen.

Our discussions were usually about the conditions in the camp, the progress of the war but, most often, we talked about our homes and about food. Each one recalled in minute details the wonderful meals that their mother had cooked, especially for the holidays and for other celebrations.

I recall one incident that is descriptive of our inability to be shocked by anything. During the fall, a young couple came to the camp. He was tall, dark and handsome, she was a beautiful blond blue-eyed girl. They were a most striking couple. Both of them were totally incapable of adapting to the stark realities of the camp, and very soon they started to go downhill. The young man became ill with typhus and he was brought to the stable to keep him warm. He lay a few feet from us, obviously in the last hours of his life. He was unconscious, his body was covered with rags and lice were crawling on his eyes. We went on with our conversation, every now and then checking if he was still alive. Some of us even envied his nonviolent ending.

Later in the winter, they moved us from the unheated barracks to a peasant hut. Seven girls lived in one room. I was the youngest working girl and one girl, a year or two younger than I, was hiding out with us. There was also one family consisting of five adults. One of the girls who was slightly handicapped physically was our cook. Firewood for cooking was hard to come by, even though forests surrounded the village, because it was forbidden to cut down any trees. One evening, when our firewood was all but gone, one of the girls and I decided to take a chance and cut down a tree in the forest.

After dark, we stole our way to the edge of the forest; it

was a bright starry night and the snow crunched under our feet. We selected a suitable tree and proceeded to cut it down. Each blow with the ax reverberated throughout the forest, or so it seemed to us. We managed to cut down the tree and now we had to bring it back without being detected. It was still dark when we almost made it to our hut but, as we were crossing a small brook, my end of the tree fell down and broke the thin ice on the brook. I tried desperately to lift it, but my fingers were numb from the cold. A new day was about to break and we had to get back to the hut. Finally, I managed to get a hold of my end of the tree and we made it! We hid the tree in the snow under the window. Though tired and cold we had been successful and were greeted with relief and joy.

The typhus epidemic took its toll in our camp. One day Fritzka and I tried to hitch a ride to work with a friend as he drove by on a horse-drawn sled. He motioned to us not to sit down, even though the sled seemed to be empty. We were puzzled; R. had always been helpful and friendly. Later, we found out that on the sled covered with straw were two bodies of our people who had died that night. Our friend was trying to get them out of the camp and bury them secretly, without the authorities discovering how bad the situation in the camp really was. It was common practice for the police to regularly sweep through the camp and shoot sick people.

One night, covered only with our thin clothes, I felt that Fritzka was burning up. I did not need a medical diagnosis to know that she had typhus. I tried to cool her burning forehead with snow, before leaving for work. We were working outdoors at the threshing machine. Around noontime we heard shots in the camp. The Ukrainian police had swept through the barracks shooting all sick people. A friend told me that when they came to our hut, they asked him to help Fritzka get down from the bunk. He tried to help her put on her shoes but she looked at him and said: "where I am going I don't need any shoes". With her head held high, this fifteen-year-old girl walked out unaided and was shot in front of our hut. Only a dirty brown stain remained when I came back from work. Fritzka was no more...

It was hard to go on but the news of the German defeat at Stalingrad and the wish to bear witness and see the killers punished helped me get through another day.

In January, a group of Hungarian Jewish men came through our camp. They had been attached to the Hungarian army as auxiliary troops, to dig ditches etc. This was a forced labor battalion and they did not carry any weapons. When the men realized that they had come upon a group of Jews, they could hardly believe it. They told us that they had marched through much of the Ukraine without encountering any Jews. They were so happy to see us and we, of course, also rejoiced at their presence. A few quick romances developed. One of our girls left with the Jewish boys. They dressed her in a Hungarian army uniform and tried to smuggle her out of the camp. To our great sorrow we heard that she was discovered during an inspection before crossing the bridge over the Dniester River and was shot.

We began to see long convoys of horse-drawn carriages with Ukrainians and Russians who had collaborated with the Germans and were now fleeing with the retreating German armies. The German retreat was picking up greater steam day by day. We heard the booms of the great Soviet rockets, the "katushas", and our guards confirmed that the front was moving closer but they assured us that they would kill us all before the Russians could reach our camp. The "Banderovcys", ultra-nationalist Ukrainian armed groups, were a constant threat to us. We heard that they had held a meeting and decided to kill all Jews, so as not to leave any witnesses. They also encouraged the local peasants to do the same.

We were in mortal danger from these groups. They overran some of our camps and murdered many Jews.

At this point, the Gestapo was not much in evidence. They were too busy looting and dispatching their booty to Germany. They had exhibited great bravery murdering defenseless innocent people but, I guess, they were not too keen to confront the Soviet army.

What happened then was a curious paradox: the German camp commander was protecting us from the Ukrainian mobs. The Germans realized that they were loosing the war and some of them, I guess, got tired of the killings. The camp commander told all the Jewish workers to assemble in the largest camp in Tluste where he would protect us from the Ukrainian thugs. We also felt, that there was greater safety, in being all together.

More and more German troops were passing through the town and spending a day or two there, before marching further west. Some of them put their horses in our stables. The withdrawal was in full force. The camp was very crowded; there was not enough room in the barracks. Some nights I slept in the stable, since it was also the warmest place. One day, when I woke up in the stable, I saw a young German soldier in front of me. I froze. He pulled out of his pocket a candy bar and offered it to me; he kept telling me in German that it was all right, I should not be afraid to accept it. Even though I was starved, I refused to take the chocolate bar from him. I had such a deep hatred for the Germans, thinking that they cannot wash away the blood on their hands with a candy bar. But it took all my will power to do so.

During the last days of the German occupation, some of us were working at the railroad station, loading everything movable onto flatbed train cars going to Germany. The trains were moving slowly as we loaded sacks of flour, and all kinds of grains, potatoes, live pigs and chickens. Next to the railroad station, was a huge mountain of grain. The Germans did not have sufficient time to load it, so they poured gasoline on it and set it on fire.

Liberation

On March 27, 1944, quite suddenly, Soviet troops entered the town of Tluste and liberated the camp. People cried and hugged each other and some tried to kiss the soldiers. We could not believe that we were finally free! With that first rush of freedom came also the sobering realization, that we were merely a few remnants of our families and our communities. The Russian soldiers told us that they had traveled thousands of miles but had never seen a Jewish camp. Some even wondered whether we might be German collaborators. That suspicion dissipated quickly and they were very nice to us. Unfortunately, only half an hour after the liberation and before we could take a deep breath of freedom, several German Stuka planes bombed our camp. The wooden barracks burned quickly and many people died in the fire. Many were also hit by machine-gun fire as they tried to flee from the burning barracks.

Wounded and moaning people were everywhere. I was asked to go immediately to one of the barracks to help a wounded girl. She lay on the floor on a pile of straw, moaning softly; the stench of burned flesh was terrible. I gently tried to take off her cover to bandage her wounds but I saw a gaping hole where her chest had been. I tried to comfort her and told her that we would take her to a Russian field hospital. She merely asked me to hold her hand and whispered that it was too late for her. I had known that girl; we had called her our nightingale because on quiet evenings, she used to sing for us, songs about home and family. Now her voice was stilled forever...

Our sudden liberation was due to the fact that a large

German army had been encircled around the city of Tarnopol. The Soviets advanced so rapidly that the Gestapo and the Ukrainian police had no time to eliminate the camp. On the second or third day of liberation, we heard that the German army was breaking out of the encirclement and that now the Russians were retreating. We started running after the Russian tanks and army trucks on that bitterly cold day. We were all poorly clothed; I had wooden shoes on, others wrapped their feet with rags. We dragged along as best we could and at nightfall we reached the town of Buczacz. We found an empty house there, lay down totally exhausted on the cold floor and fell asleep. In the middle of the night, we heard the rumbling of Russian tanks and armored cars leaving the town.

We were terrified that we might fall again into German hands, got up and started to follow the Russian tanks and trucks. It was a pitch-dark night, snow was falling heavily and it was very cold. A few hundred emaciated and totally bedraggled Jews were running as best they could after the army vehicles. I was slipping and sliding in my wooden shoes on those icy roads, and could not keep up very well. We found ourselves in some woods; the scene was chaotic with the Russian army withdrawing east along on the road. We were running behind them, and from each side Banderovcys (Ukrainian Nationalists) and German soldiers were shooting at the Russians and at us. At one point, a Russian soldier on a tank extended his hand and pulled me up unto the tank. What happened next is a complete blank. Some time later, the straggling camp inmates found me half-frozen, sitting propped up next to an overturned tank. I don't know what happened but I must have been caught in a battle.

My friends woke me up and tried to help me walk, but in fact they just dragged me with them to the next town of Podvolochisk, on the former Polish-Russian border. There, the Russians were in complete control and we finally felt free and safe. Did I say free and safe? Free, from the

German terror yes, but safe, hardly. We, the pitiful remnant of our communities, were unwelcome in our former homes. We heard many times from the local people that the only good thing the Germans did was to kill the Jews.

A few of us from the camp who had reached Podwoloczysk found an empty house and took it over. We felt safe knowing that a few Russian officers were billeted across the hall. Now began the daily struggle for survival and the terrible realization how few of us had survived. We did not feel safe going to the villages to seek food, but instead went to the Russian field kitchens and asked for food. They usually gave us some leftover soup or a piece of bread. It was a daily task and we all took turns doing it.

This was the spring of 1944, and I was not quite sixteen years old. During the entire period in the ghetto and the labor camp most of the women did not menstruate and neither did I. Suddenly, it started again, not a welcome event under these dire circumstances. How strange though, nature can be!

We were all waiting impatiently to hear that our towns had been liberated and that it was now safe for us to return home and look for family and friends who survived.

One day, a Russian soldier came to our room and said that his commanding officer had sent him to look for a blond girl whom he had seen at the field kitchen. He finally spotted me and said that his officer asked him to bring food and vodka for us, that he would come later and we would have a party. Soon afterwards, an officer from one of the Central Asian Republics came riding on a horse, decked out with a Persian style rug under the saddle. He wore a black cape and across his chest was a bandoleer of bullets, a sight that seemed to me as from the stories of the Arabian nights.

More soldiers arrived with food and drinks. Someone brought an accordion and the party was in full swing. The officer insisted that I sit next to him. He told me how much he liked me, and that he wanted to marry me. Everyone had a good time and, for the first time since the war, there was plenty of food to eat. As the evening progressed, I was beginning to feel more and more apprehensive.

When I stepped outside for a moment, one of the Russian officers who lived next door, saw me. He had heard all the commotion in our room and he took me aside to talk to me. He asked whether I knew what "voyennaya polevaya zhena" (a war bride) meant. I said I did not know. He explained that what this officer had in mind was to use me and drop me in the next town. He urged me to get away. He happened to be an older Jewish man and he was very kind to me. I hid in a deserted hut until the party broke up, late that night. I was told the next day, that "my" officer had become quite drunk and was very angry that he could not find his "dyewuchka" – his girl. One more time near disaster was avoided...

My hatred for the Germans consumed me. I wanted revenge for all the suffering, for the innocent blood they had spilled. I had seen women in the Soviet army and, without telling anybody, I decided to enlist. I had passed for eighteen in the camp, so I thought that I could do it again. All I wanted was a gun in my hands.

I found the military command headquarters located on the outskirts of town in a small peasant hut. I went in and told the soldier on duty, that I wanted to enlist in the army. He did not seem shocked or surprised and asked me to wait for the commanding officer. I waited for quite a long time and it started getting dark. Since there was a curfew in town, I was afraid that I would not have enough time to return to my friends. Every time I tried to leave, the soldier kept reassuring me that the commanding officer would come soon, and he would make the proper arrangements for my enlistment. As night fell, I was told that I would have to wait till the next day. I was led to a little room in a peasant's hut and was told I could spend there the night.

I felt uneasy, but since there was a curfew, I had no choice. I sat on the bed and tried to rest. Suddenly I heard the door open and a young soldier walked in. He tried to lie down next to me and make love. I spent the whole night crying and begging him to leave me alone. He was a very young boy, not a vicious rapist. When he realized how young I really was, not quite sixteen, and frightened, he stopped being aggressive and just simply held me in his arms and fell asleep. In the morning he gave me a loaf of bread and a box of sardines. I left the little hut, saddened but wiser and realized how naïve I had been!

I started walking back to my friends. I had not eaten the previous day and did not sleep much that night. Suddenly, I felt very weak and collapsed. I don't know how long I lay on that muddy road. Many people must have passed by but nobody tried to help. I was sure that the end had now come. I looked up at the sky and the white clouds above. The puddles of water glistened with many colors from the oil spilled on the road by military vehicles. I thought, at least I shall die free. I don't know how long I lay there, but eventually I recovered and returned to "our" house. I gave my friends the loaf of bread and the can of sardines, but did not tell anyone what had happened. I was too ashamed of my naiveté.

We waited in Podvoloczysk another week, until we heard that our area was finally free of Germans. We started hitchhiking home with Russian soldiers. The first town we returned to was Tluste, the hometown of some of my friends. We found out that the old and sick people, who could not run away with us, were killed when the Germans reoccupied Tluste. I then hitchhiked to Horodenka. When the army truck stopped in the center of town, I went down and started walking towards our house. I saw from afar that our house was a ruin, most probably destroyed during the last bombing of Horodenka by the Germans. It was less than three years since I left my hometown; the buildings were the same but the town had changed completely. Only a handful of Jews returned to Horodenka and they warned me not to stay there overnight, since the local population was very hostile and some returning Jews were murdered in neighboring towns.

My hope that Uncle Jacob and his wife might have survived was unfortunately dashed. I heard rumors my uncle, his wife and the dentist Zenezib, had been killed by the peasant who hid them.

I walked through the streets of the former ghetto that was once teeming with Jews, but now, not a single Jewish face could be seen. Most of the Jewish houses were occupied by Poles and Ukrainians. Some stood desolate and empty; on the doors of some one could still see the "Mezuzot" (small metal boxes containing a scroll with a prayer in Hebrew that most Jews affixed to their front doors). I was afraid to go to my grandmother's house that had been the last home for our entire family, because the new occupants might think that I had come to reclaim my home and I had little doubt about the reception awaiting me. With a heavy heart I left my hometown of Horodenka, not to return there for fifty-three years.

I returned to Tluste where my friends were. Every day was a struggle for survival because of the scarcity of food. We heard that across the border in Romania conditions were much better. A few of us hit the road again and hitched a ride with some Russian army trucks to Romania. At that time, the war was still on and there were no borders between the former Polish territory and the Romanian province of Bucovina. After the war, all these territories were incorporated in the Ukrainian Soviet Republic. We arrived outside Czernowitz, the provincial capital, hungry and exhausted, only to find out that the city had been closed to refugees. We waited till nightfall and with the help of a guide waded across the Pruth River and entered the city of Czernowitz. Someone led us to an empty apartment where, totally exhausted, we lay down on the floor and fell asleep.

Czernowitz

When I woke up the next morning, a bright sun was shining through the window. I looked out and could not believe my eyes: what I saw was a beautiful city, seemingly untouched by war. Streetcars were running, and women with make-up and wearing neat dresses and high heels were walking in the street. I did not know that a world like that still existed. I was only thirty or forty miles from the towns we had left, but it seemed that I found myself on an entirely different planet.

We went down, stood bewildered at a street corner and were immediately surrounded by some of the townspeople. Apparently, we were one of the first groups to have come from across the border. In our wooden shoes and dirty rags we must have been a bizarre sight. Many Jews in Czernowitz had relatives in Poland and they were eager to know from what cities we had come and what we knew about their loved ones. Sadly, they soon learned that we did not bring good news.

It turned out that one of the men in the group of local people was a cousin of my mother's and he took me home with him. His wife was rather startled by my appearance. Aunt Etelka, as I came to call her, proceeded to burn my filthy clothes and scrubbed me from head to toe. How can I describe the incredible pleasure of that first bath? To be able to finally wash away the accumulated dirt and grime of the past years and to look forward to a clean bed without the constant torture of lice!

I used to dream in the camp of sleeping just one more time in a clean bed and not feel hungry before I died. As it developed, sleep did not come easy because nightmares troubled me almost nightly.

I stood before the bathroom mirror in total shock. I had not seen a mirror in a long time and I remembered my child's face, but when did I grow up? How did I age so much beyond my years? My long blond hair had turned into a mess of blond curls, after I lost all my hair during my bout with typhus. I was not a child anymore.

It was very difficult to learn to live again, as hope faded gradually that any members of my family might have survived. There were no psychologists there to help me deal with my traumas. Everyone told me how lucky I was to be alive and how happy they felt for me. I smiled and thanked them, but inside me I felt hollow and was deeply wounded. Those invisible scars would not heal for a long, long time.

As news spread in the apartment house that someone has come from the camps across the border, neighbors began arriving and asked questions. Most people in Czernowitz spoke German, not my favorite language, and when I tried to tell them as best I could what had happened in Poland, few understood and even fewer believed me. One woman looked at me and said: "it could not have been so bad there, considering how well she looks". In spite of my severe malnutrition, she mistook my oval face and high cheekbones for someone well nourished. I did not tell many stories after that.

The first few days in Czernowitz were quite overwhelming. My aunt spoke only German and it was hard getting used to hearing German, the language of the murderers, all around me. My uncle spoke some Polish and this helped.

I was in very poor physical condition, with boils on my arms and legs. My gums were bleeding profusely when I tried to chew a piece of bread. I was very hungry all the time, ate everything that was offered and could not wait for the next meal.

A few weeks later, I heard that my cousin Julia Rosenbaum had survived on Aryan papers and had returned to Zaleszczyki. Once again, I stood on the main highway and hitched a ride with an army truck to Zaleszczyki. We had a very sad reunion. She told me of her harrowing experiences in the Ukraine where, at one point, she passed as an ethnic German, but after the liberation was arrested by the Soviets who did not believe that she was indeed Jewish. I told her when and how her mother and sister perished and the fate of our entire family. Unexpectedly, a telegram arrived from the Soviet military informing her that her father, a physician who had been drafted by the Soviets at the beginning of the war, was killed in the battle of Stalingrad. She had decided to go to Palestine and had visited the mass grave at the cemetery in Tluste, where her mother and sister were buried. There, she gathered a bit of soil to take along with her. Here we were, the two of us, the only survivors of my father's and mother's families, preparing to leave our homeland forever...

I returned to Czernowitz where, after years of terror and starvation, I slowly began to regain my health. The wounds on my legs and arms healed, my gums stopped bleeding, but I was still continuously hungry, no matter how much I ate. Food was still scarce, so I had to be careful not to eat more than my share. Perhaps more serious than the obvious physical health problems were the deep emotional wounds that would not heal. I often woke up screaming at night, a recurring dream being capture by the Germans. This lasted for many years and still happens, occasionally. I never saw a doctor or a psychologist about this; no one realized then how deeply traumatized the survivors were.

When schools reopened in September, I was enrolled in a Russian school. I was very conscious of the fact that I had lost many years of schooling and now needed to catch up, yet everything we studied seemed trivial and not relevant to my life. How could I concentrate on poetry and literature after the events of the recent past? Nothing made sense. I obviously did not know, at the time, what Theodor Adorno was to say later: "...writing poetry after Auschwitz is barbaric..." The only thing I wanted answered was "WHY", why the hatred, why the carnage, but the teachers never spoke about that.

I wound up in a class with students of my own age. Though I had lost three years of schooling, I could keep up with them scholastically because it was easier for me to understand Russian, a Slavic language related to my native Polish. Many other students had not attended school regularly during the war, and they were also trying to catch up. Even though I was the same age as they were, I felt much older, as if I had already lived many lives. I could not find a common language with these young people, I never spoke of my past, and they never asked me about it.

A family from Horodenka asked me if I could tutor their little girl in basic reading, writing and math. The child could not attend school. She spoke very little, even with her parents, and did not communicate with other people. This beautiful little girl, seven or eight years old, had been hidden during the German occupation in a cellar where she was allowed to speak only in whispers. She seemed to be shell-shocked, could not concentrate and was very hard to reach. Little by little she started to communicate with me. I don't know how much I was able to teach her but her parents were very pleased that she gradually opened up to me. This was my first attempt at teaching, a vocation I was to practice later in life. I often wondered what became of that child.

One day, I was walking in the city when a Russian policeman stopped me and asked me for my papers. Since I had none, I wound up at the police station. There, I was brought before an official sitting behind a big desk. He also asked me for my papers, the whereabouts of my parents, my place of origin, etc. I was then told that I was not allowed to live in this city and was placed under arrest.

I was furious and let go with some nasty curses, telling him: "I have survived the German camps and I shall also survive you bastards".

In the meantime, some neighbors told my aunt that they had seen me being led to the police station. My aunt did not speak Russian, but a neighbor who had some knowledge of the language volunteered to go with her to the police station to my rescue. The neighbor started pleading with the officer to let me go. In her poor Russian she referred to me as a baby. The Russian officer started to laugh and said: "if a baby like this falls on your foot, it could break your toe". I laughed as well, since I understood the joke. Anyway, the ice was broken and he let me go, admonishing me not to have such a big mouth in the future. I guess he started to feel uncomfortable with too many people having become involved; the Russian police preferred to work in secrecy.

I learned later that the police were rounding up orphaned children who were then shipped off to the Donbas coalmines. The word "prostitutes" was written in big letters on the cattle cars carrying those poor people.

My uncle and aunt insisted that it was too dangerous for me to walk around town without papers, so they decided to adopt me. They registered me with the authorities as their natural daughter. I felt I was too old for adoption and I resented to have to change my name I was deeply troubled since I felt that, all that was left of my former life, was my name. What further added to my unease was the fact that my uncle and aunt registered me one year younger, because they had not been married long enough to have a daughter my age.

On May 8, 1945, VE-Day, the most brutal war in Europe was over. As the news reached us, spontaneous celebrations broke out all over town. Loudspeakers blared patriotic speeches and martial music. There was dancing in the streets and, obviously, the Russian soldiers who suffered enormous casualties in this war were the happiest.

I was also glad that the carnage had stopped, but I was feeling quite desolate in the midst of all that rejoicing. I was now all alone, the people I loved and the friends I cherished were gone forever and my home, my little Jewish "shtetl", had vanished.

It learned only gradually about the magnitude of the destruction of Europe's Jewry. Hitler lost the war, but so did we. Great Jewish centers of learning, scholars, writers and artists were no more. For the few survivors, Poland had become one big cemetery, a cemetery without gravestones, a cemetery in the sky....

I often asked myself how could I continue living in a world where everything reminded me of my family, my home and my friends. How to go on? What was the point? The pain was so great...

I remember passing a house in our neighborhood whence came sounds of a piano with white curtains billowing in the open window. I felt such a deep pain realizing that I shall never hear my father or my brother play the flute again. There was life all around me but I felt dead inside.

After the war ended there was an exchange of populations between Poland and the USSR. Polish citizens were allowed to emigrate to Poland and my uncle saw this as an opportunity to leave the Soviet Union and we were all allowed to leave. The Soviet army did liberate us from Hitler, but we had no desire to live under the communist regime, hoping to emigrate to Palestine, the United States, or Canada.

I stopped going to school and spent my days on the city's open market hawking the family's possessions. It seemed that all the Jews of Czernowitz were at that market, trying to sell as many of their household goods as they could, before leaving the city. Most Jews and Poles tried to leave, some going to Romania, some to Poland or other countries in the West.

We stood for hours outside the emigration office, waiting to hear our names called and then learn about the date of our departure.

Return to Poland

When our turn finally came to leave, we packed a few things to take with us and made our way to the railroad station. The place was mobbed, but eventually we were assigned to an open railroad car. Each family staked out a little corner on the straw-covered floor. Occasionally, sparks from the engine ignited the straw. It seemed that entire villages with their priests were being evacuated together. They sang patriotic Polish songs and seemed to be quite happy to be resettled in Poland, in formerly German territories. The few Polish Jews huddled together, quite apprehensive about what they would find at the end of this journey.

Our train was often sidetracked, and sometimes we waited for hours. After what seemed like a long journey, we arrived in Prague. We did not see very much of this beautiful city; we were allowed to get off only long enough to buy food from passing vendors. Eventually, we arrived in the city of Gliwice (Gleiwitz), formerly in German Upper Silesia. We were assigned to an apartment abandoned by Germans that we shared with another Jewish family. Life was slowly returning to normal, the streetcars started running again and the post office was operating. My uncle and aunt wrote to their relatives in the U.S. and I also tried to get in touch with an aunt, my father's sister, who lived in New York. Mail was not yet being delivered and had to be picked up at the main regional post office in Bytom. I made frequent trips to that town, awaiting a letter from America.

The political situation in Poland immediately after the war was quite unsettled. It became apparent that a communist form of government was being imposed by the Soviets. Some of the leaders of the Polish government-in-exile in London did return but they were soon squeezed out by the communists. The Russian military presence was very much in evidence. We had no desire to live again under communist rule and therefore planned to leave Poland.

A few Jews were trickling back from German camps. A Jewish center was established in an abandoned building. We went there frequently, hoping to find a familiar face, perhaps even a lost relative. One wall in the center was covered with notes from people looking for their loved ones. The notes became more numerous with time and, occasionally we witnessed a happy reunion, but those were few and far between. When a letter finally arrived from my aunt in New York, I opened it with trembling hands; she was, after all, my closest living relative. I was surprised that her husband wrote the letter and the more I read the more depressed I became. In my letter I wrote what had happened to our family during the war. My uncle now wrote not to ever mention those troubling events because that upset my aunt too much. I was greatly saddened, they did not even want to know what happened!

Our situation in Poland was becoming increasingly more difficult. The few survivors were not welcome in our country of birth. The news of the massacre by Poles of 42 Jews in Kielce, a city not far away from where we lived, was a terrible shock. We often heard Poles opining that the only good thing Hitler had done was to get rid of the Jews. Most of the Jewish survivors in Poland did not need any more convincing to make every effort to leave the country as soon as possible. My aunt in New York urged me to go to the American Consul in Warsaw and apply for a visa to the U.S.A.

My uncle and I traveled to Warsaw. As we approached the city, we were shocked by the sight that met our eyes: most of the city was leveled. Some of the main avenues, like Aleja Jerozolimska, had been cleared of rubble but the buildings on either side were completely demolished. The city looked like a strange moonscape.

With some difficulty we located the American Consulate in Praga, one of the suburbs of Warsaw across the Vistula River. The consulate was located in one of the few buildings that were still standing. Long lines of applicants stretched outside the building. We filled out an application and were told that we would be notified if and when our visas would be granted.

Two events occurred that changed the direction of my life.

While we were waiting impatiently to leave the country, we began to hear about the "shlichim", young Jews from Palestine, who were trying to help the Jewish survivors to emigrate to Palestine. It was a lifeline for others and me. Somewhere in this world we were still wanted! I started taking Hebrew lessons with two other girls from an elderly Jewish man. I dreamed of living on a Kibbutz (a collective farm) for which my work during the war had certainly prepared me. I hoped to find a surrogate family among people who, like me, had lost their families. The dream of having a place of our own and not be driven from one country to another, would finally become a reality. As it turned out, I did not emigrate to Palestine, but I remained all my life a committed Zionist and later became a teacher of Hebrew.

At that time, Palestine was still a British mandate, and aunt Ethelka insisted that knowledge of English was very important. She was acquainted with a lady from Czernowitz whose son knew English and arranged for me to take lessons. That is how I met my future husband, Fred. At first, we had no common language, I spoke only Polish, he spoke German (though he had grown up in Romania), English, French, Russian but not Polish! We did not hit it off very well in the beginning. The "exercises for translation" that he assigned me were not very conducive to romance.

We communicated somehow in my poor German, but that meant that we could not talk in public places in Poland, since Fred risked opprobrium being taken for a German. What an irony! On occasion, he amused my friends with his attempts to speak Polish. I was quite impressed with this young man. He was the most intelligent boy I had ever met. He had the good fortune of being able to study in Czernowitz. His teachers were some of the Jewish professors in the city who were not allowed to teach in schools during the war. Fred and the other three young men who had studied with him later immigrated to different countries and all had brilliant careers, as professors, doctors, and engineers. My husband became a professor of nuclear engineering at Georgia Tech and M.I.T. But that came much later and in the meantime our ways parted.

The Polish quota for immigration to the U.S. was very small, and it became clear that it might take years to be able to emigrate there. It was rumored that if one could make it to the American zone in Germany, things could be speeded up. My uncle and aunt wanted to go to America but I had my heart set on Palestine, though Israel was not yet created.

Once again, we packed our few meager possessions and started on another journey into the unknown. I left Poland, where our people had lived for a thousand years, with a sense of relief but also of bitterness, recalling the behavior of our Polish fellow citizens during the last trying years. It is true that a number of Jewish survivors owe their lives to a few courageous Poles but, sadly, even today, some of those who helped to hide Jews do not want their neighbors to know about it. It is no honor in Poland to have saved a Jewish life!

The Waiting Room in Germany

We arrived in Fürth in the American zone of Germany and proceeded to the DP camp (displaced persons camp) there. The camp, consisting of a couple of streets lined with small houses, seemed to me like a ghetto. We stood for a while with our bundles on a street corner, until we were assigned some living quarters. The place was small with very few amenities, but we did not care, since we thought that we would be able to leave this place soon.

We learned quickly that reaching either destination, Palestine or the U.S., was not going to be easy. The British had essentially blocked legal Jewish immigration to Palestine. Those who managed to reach its shores, often in vessels that were not seaworthy, were arrested in sight of their "Promised Land" and interned on Cyprus. The anger and desperation in the displaced persons camps was palpable. Many former concentration camp inmates, especially those who were ill with tuberculosis and other ailments could not get permission to immigrate to many countries. With doors closed, for many people the only hope was Palestine.

The news that the ship "Exodus", which had sailed from a French port near Marseilles on July 11, 1947, was escorted by British destroyers and then rammed by them as it approached the coast of Palestine, caused great consternation and anger, not only among the refugees, but also around the world. On that ship were 4,515 immigrants, including 655 children. The immigrants fought with the soldiers who tried to remove them from the ship; two were killed and thirty were wounded. Eventually, the immigrants were transferred onto prison ships bound for France but the French refused to force them off the boat. On August 22, the ship left for the port of Hamburg, in the British zone, where the immigrants were removed by force and placed in camps. The fact that Jews had been forced to return to Germany to live among the murderers of our people in the country responsible for the greatest slaughter of our people in history appalled, angered and saddened all of us. We wondered whether there was any place on this planet where we belonged.

We had to settle down in Fürth for what might be a long wait. My uncle managed to find an apartment in the center of the city. The AJDC and HIAS (Jewish relief agencies) as well as UNRRA (United Nations Relief and Rehabilitation Administration) were already active in town. We regularly received food packages but some of the foods puzzled us. A brown spread in a jar was called butter. We had never seen peanut butter before, so some people were complaining that the Americans thought that brown butter, rather than the real thing, was good enough for us. As the Passover holidays were approaching, boxes of "matzos" (unleavened bread) arrived. Most of us were deeply moved, that somewhere, far away, there were people who cared about us.

A Jewish Community Center was organized where food, clothing and household goods were distributed to the refugees. In the camp, people organized a makeshift synagogue in an army Quonset hut and services were held regularly. An American Jewish chaplain officiated at the High Holiday services.

It was quite a revelation for me to observe the "Herrenvolk" (master race) on their home turf after their defeat. They no longer strutted around as arrogantly as they did in my town during the war. Then, a Jew could be killed for not getting off the sidewalk fast enough and for not bowing before them. Our German landlady assured us that she was never a Nazi, as did most of the Germans at the time. One wondered where those who had crowded the huge stadium at Nuremberg screaming their adoration for the Führer had gone. Most of the "Fräuleins" could be had for a pack of cigarettes or a bit of Nescafe. How have the mighty fallen! Every now and then you could see a grand-mother wheeling a bi-racial baby in the park. I could not help wondering how this poor child would fare in this racist society and I hoped that his daddy would take him some day to America.

The denazification process was in full swing but what a farce it was! Most of the policemen who had served under the Nazis, including some who had participated in the mass murder of Jews, were quickly cleared and again became policemen in the new Germany. The old judges who had enforced the Nuremberg laws were again presiding in the courts of law. A few high profile Nazis were sentenced to death and some went to jail, but most went on with their lives without ever answering for their crimes in a court of law.

When the Nuremberg trials began I received a pass from the Polish delegation and was able to attend one of the sessions. Each country that had been occupied by the Germans had a representative at Nuremberg. How can I describe my feelings when I faced Göring and all the other top Nazis being escorted by the MPs into the Hall of Justice? I felt a deep hatred, loathing and revulsion looking at those totally unremarkable ugly faces. Were these the faces of evil? Their orders had caused so much suffering and the deaths of millions of innocent people. Many years later, Eichmann's defense was that he had only followed the orders of these criminals. They wore clean suits, looked well fed, and most of them remained unrepentant to the end.

I followed the proceedings of the trial day by day and read the editorials in some German papers, challenging the right of the Allies to try these murderers.

[A few years ago I had the privilege of meeting and serving

on the same panel with Mr. Whitney R. Harris, who served at Nuremberg as the Executive Trial Counsel to Justice Jackson, the chief U.S. Prosecutor. Mr. Harris who is the author of "Tyranny on Trial" later discussed with us the background of the trial. It was a very emotional event for me.]

Years later I learned how the Vatican had helped some of the most notorious criminals flee to South America and thus escape justice.

When I walked on the streets of Fürth and saw a German of military age, I always wondered whether he could have been the one who had pulled the trigger on my brother. My only social contacts at the time were with my friends in the DP camp. Each one of them had his own story of tragedy and loss. Only a few of my contemporaries had parents or siblings. We became a close-knit group and most of us hoped to soon reach Palestine. In 1946, a few Palestinian Jews arrived in the camp where they organized Hebrew classes and encouraged us not to give up the struggle to reach Palestine. Nobody wished to remain in Germany and emigration was paramount in our minds.

Since it seemed that I was wasting my time again, my aunt insisted that I attend school. German schools were the only schools available to me. In spite of my strong resentment of everything German, I realized that I had no choice. Thus started my career as the only Jewish student in the "Mädchen Oberschule" – a girls' high school, in Fürth. Obviously, I felt strange and totally alienated from my fellow students, most of them former members of the "Hitler Jugend". I went to classes, I studied, and I went home. During recess I ate lunch by myself. After classes I had a whole bevy of private tutors: I studied German, English, Latin, math and science. I worked hard trying to make up for all the lost years of schooling. Of course, I spoke with some of the classmates, but I had no personal or social ties with any of them. Some of the girls invited me to their parties, especially at Fasching (carnival) time, when they dressed up in costumes and partied all night, but I always turned down their invitations. I could not forget for a moment, that only a few short years back some of their grandfathers, fathers, or brothers could have worn the SS uniforms and had participated in mass murder.

One girl, in particular, stands out in my mind. Inge Müller was a tall and beautiful blond girl. I liked her and we used to chat during the recess. She told me that her father had been killed on the eastern front. At that time, I found it impossible to feel any sympathy for her. I could not help wondering if her father could have been the Mr. Müller who had terrorized my family and at one point put a gun to my mother's head urging her to confess that an Aryan fathered me. I was aware that the name Müller was as popular in Germany as Smith was in America, but suspicion lingered on. The unbridgeable chasm remained.

Some of the girls in my class were quite musical and they used to get together for musical evenings and, on occasion, they invited me to join them. One would think that music, the universal language that knows no frontiers, could have bridged the gap between us, but I could not help thinking that while the slaughters were being perpetrated, many Germans still listened to Beethoven's "Ninth's Symphony", – "Alle Menschen werden Brüder" (All men shall be brothers), but these words did not move them or mitigate their brutal behavior towards their fellow men. I never attended these musical evenings.

Fred, my future husband, was at the time studying Chemistry at the Technical University in Munich. We renewed our friendship and he used to come to Fürth quite often. We attended theater, concerts and operas. On many occasions, our meager budgets allowed only for standing room tickets on the top balcony. A new world had opened for me. Fred helped me discover French literature, which he loved, and we visited museums and took long walks in parks. I read ravenously, eager to learn about life and about the world beyond concentration camps.

The young people in the DP camps awaiting emigration were idle and restless and the black market enticed some of them. They came out of the concentration camps destitute and were looking for a chance to make some money. American cigarettes were the preferred currency. A pound of coffee could be bartered for a fancy sets of Rosenthal china or a sterling silver set. These were indeed strange times. But there were also many young Jews who sought to acquire in Germany only one thing: an education. They came from various countries and spoke many different languages. At the Jewish Students Union in Munich the unofficial language was Polish, since most of the students had come from Poland. These students felt strongly that Germany owed them an education. After all, many German universities and research institutions had once been enriched by the achievements of Jewish professors and scientists.

I received a government stipend of 80 marks and during the summer vacation I was sent to Garmisch Partenkirchen in the beautiful Bavarian Alps region. I could not help wondering how a country of such natural beauty and cultural wealth could have fallen so quickly under the spell of a brutal dictator. Why would a people who enjoyed such a high standard of living find it necessary to come to my small poor town of Horodenka to rob and pillage?

I shall always remember the day of May 15, 1948, when the news reached us that David Ben Gurion had proclaimed an independent Jewish state, to be called Israel. The first law to be promulgated was the Law of Return. Any Jew anywhere in the world now had a home, a place where he was welcome, a haven from oppression, and a land where Jews can live in freedom and be masters of their own destiny. These were heady days, but also days filled with great worry and concern when five Arab countries invaded Israel on the day it declared it's independence. We heard about heavy battles and truces that did not last long and we feared for our relatives and friends who were already in Israel.

Travel to Israel was difficult; the whole country was a war zone. I did register with the Israeli recruiting team in the Fürth DP camp, as did most other young people; I was given a medical exam, was declared fit, and was told to await orders.

The political situation in Europe was worsening with relations between the Allies and the Soviets becoming strained. The Soviets blockaded the supply routes to the Western sectors of Berlin and the allied airlift started in September 1948. Tensions were very high and the talk of war was heard again. Years later, when I read President Truman's biography I realized how real the threat had been. The one thing that terrified me more than anything else was being caught in Europe in another war.

I had started to correspond with my mother's cousin, Toby Sadofsky, in Peekskill, N.Y. She offered to send me an affidavit indicating that, if I were admitted to the US, I could live with her and not became a burden to the state. She ran a tourist house and she stated that I would be employed as a maid. I thanked her and asked her to go ahead. Early in 1949, the emigration authorities notified me that my immigration papers had arrived and that I could leave in March. That put me in a quandary since I was preparing for the "Abitur" (high school graduation exam). Passing this exam would have given me one or two years of college credit in the U.S., but I decided not to delay my departure. In March I traveled to Bremen, waited there a few days and on March 23, 1949, boarded the SS Marine Flasher bound for New York.

It was the first time I had seen the sea and the first time I traveled by ship. As the ship eased out of the harbor, I stood at the rail for a long time. So many contradicting emotions stirred in me: a feeling of relief that I was finally departing from this bloody continent, but I also felt sad to leave the place where my ancestors had lived for many centuries and where they are buried in unmarked graves. I also felt great anticipation and a bit of apprehension about this new phase of my life that was about to begin.

The SS Marine Flasher was an army transport ship, used after the war to ferry displaced persons to the States but, as far as I was concerned, it was a most luxurious liner. Two women shared a cabin and the first meal seemed to me like a banquet. Grapefruits and bananas, fruits I had never seen before, were served. The crew was very friendly and all went well till we reached the English Channel. There spring storms churned the water and the boat tipped and swayed in all directions. I became quite sea sick, as did most of the people on board. This did not last long and the rest of the journey was uneventful, except for one incident that had me quite alarmed. One day, I heard an announcement over the loudspeaker requesting that I report to the captain's office. My first thought was that something was wrong with my papers, that I would not be allowed to enter the country and would be sent back to Germany! I was terrified, only to learn to my great relief that Fred, my future husband, had sent a telegram welcoming me to America.

In the USA, at Last

Early morning on the sixth day, March 29, 1949, we entered New York harbor. Many people stood at the rail straining to see the Statue of Liberty; for us she was indeed a beacon of freedom and a promise for a new life. The New York skyline was quite impressive but it seemed familiar to me from all the American movies I had seen. The immigration authorities boarded the ship prior to our arrival and I was told that they would send me my "first papers" to the Peekskill address. I kept asking if I needed to have any papers with me but they assured me that it was not necessary. I was quite worried about being stopped by a policeman asking for my identification papers. I still had a lot to learn about my new country but my first lesson was not to fear everyone in a uniform.

A few distant American relatives came to welcome me at the pier. Harry Sadofsky, my cousin's husband, drove me to my new American home in Peekskill, N.Y.

My cousin lived in a nice large house. The upper stories were rented out to tourists.

There were three children in the family and the fourth was expected. The oldest, Dorris, was a beautiful girl of twelve. Nine-year-old Robert was quite amused about my accent: I had a Polish accent, but my teachers in Germany had been trained in England, so my English sounded unusually funny to him. He enthusiastically undertook to teach me proper American English. We sat on the stairs, he read stories to me and corrected my English when it was my turn to read. Little Susan, two years old with blond curls and beautiful deep blue eyes became my special darling. My cousin Toby was a kind, loving and generous person. The family received me warmly into their midst but it was not easy to adjust to the new life in America.

During my first breakfast the radio was playing, as usual, but I was getting more and more upset and, finally, asked my cousin: "what seems to be the problem here, all the talk on the radio is about Jews, Jews... what do they want from the Jews?" She laughed and explained in Polish that what I heard was an advertisement for orange juice. I was disappointed because I thought I understood the language quite well. We had studied Shakespeare in the German school but this did not prepare me for the rapid-fire American English spoken on the radio.

My cousin advised me to obtain an American high school diploma, which was essential in getting a job. On the first day at Hendrick Hudson High School I was tested for English comprehension and was placed in sixth grade. By the end of June, I made it to twelfth grade and passed the New York State Regents Examination.

My first day in an American school was quite a culture shock. The freewheeling and open discourse between students and teachers took me by surprise. We did not have to jump to attention when the teacher entered the class, as was the case in Germany. The prevailing ease and informality also delighted me. I was the only recent arrival in that school. Teachers and students were very nice to me and everyone went out of their way to be helpful.

Socially, it was difficult for me to feel comfortable with these carefree youngsters. I felt so much older and I could not relate to their youthful preoccupations with dates, fashions, sport, etc.

I dashed to New York almost every weekend to meet with friends from Europe and with Fred, who had come to the States the year before. We started dating again and this time he helped me discover New York.

That summer, after finishing high school, I had a wonderful experience: I was invited by a friend of our family to

San Diego for a visit. This was quite a discovery of America for me. It took three days to travel by train to California in those days. From Chicago to San Diego I traveled on the famed "El Capitan". When my fellow passengers found out that I had been in the country only four months, everyone tried to be helpful. I heard many stories and learned a great deal about this great country during the trip. The vastness of the land and the changing landscapes fascinated me. At one point the train stopped in the desert of Arizona and the train conductor escorted me down the train just to look around for a few minutes. San Diego was still a very small town at that time. I remember my visits to Balboa Park where, for the first time, I saw sub-tropical vegetation, such as hibiscus flowers the size of a dinner plate! We made trips to Catalina Island and across the border to Mexico. It was a lovely adventure for me, but when my middle-aged hosts began to speak of adopting me, I knew it was time to leave.

It was very difficult to get a job those days, so I took a secretarial course, hoping to enhance my chances of getting one and I recall one particular encounter. I answered a newspaper add for a job in a dry cleaning store. The owner who interviewed me was active in the local Jewish community and he had read an article in the local paper about my arrival in Peekskill. After a lengthy discussion he told me that he regretted not to offer me a job, because he was concerned that his customers might not understand me because of my accent. I was saddened, but in a way he did me a favor: I went to New York and soon landed a secretarial job.

While still in Peekskill, Fred came to visit me on the 4th of July 1949. We watched the fireworks, that exuberant display of American independence, and then sat for a long time on the porch. He proposed to me, (to this day he claims it was the other way around, that I proposed to him) and we were married on August 20, 1950.

Our first child, our beautiful son James, was born in December 1953. Our joy was boundless, we both wanted very much to have children and to build a family. Our joy was tampered by the sorrow that there were no grandparents to stand over the cradle and share our joy. No one to say "he looks just like you when you were little". Two years later our little red head, son George arrived. Tragedy revisited us again, when we lost our infant daughter Heddy to Sudden Infant Death Syndrome. Fortunately, a cuddly new baby, David, arrived a year later.

As the boys grew up, I began to look to the future and not revisit the past as often. Only in my dreams, or rather nightmares, was the past still very vivid. Bringing children into the world has been my greatest expression of faith.

THE END

Attachment 1

Visiting Horodenka, Fifty-three Years Later

by Tosia Schneider

Over half a century has passed since I walked for the last time on the streets of my hometown of Horodenka. All these years, I longed to return one more time to search for the graves of my family and to try to find out about the fate of my father, Jacob Szechter, who disappeared in the Fall of 1942.

In August 1997, my husband and I flew with LOT, Polish Air Line, from Warsaw to Lviv (Lwow, Lemberg), Ukraine. The airport was dreary and rundown. Our passports were checked several times: when we alighted from the plane, when we got off the bus at the terminal, and when the customs control began. A form had to be filled out declaring how much money and other valuables were brought into the country. The customs officials looked quite grim and frequently counted the dollar notes which had been declared. This first introduction to the grayness and depressing atmosphere of Ukraine made me wish to turn around and fly back to Warsaw. A car and driver from the Cheremosh Hotel in Chernivtzy (Czernowitz, Bukovina) waited for us and five hours later we arrived at the hotel. The hotel, less than ten years old, had the necessary amenities, was not particularly well maintained, appeared dark and depressing, and there were lapses in the availability of hot water and several blackouts. The staff, some of whom spoke English, were always very friendly.

Through survivors from Horodenka who now live in Israel, I learned about the only Jew who still lives in

Horodenka, once the home to over 5,000 Jews. Edik, "the last of the Mohicans", as he refers to himself, picked us up at the hotel and drove us to Horodenka and vicinity. In some parts, the town has changed drastically. On the main street, once lined with Jewish stores, there now stand a few non-descript Soviet-style apartment houses. The streets are in poor condition, as was the case everywhere we visited. Houses built before the war are badly in need of repairs; it seems that little was done for their upkeep, only some additions here and there, to add an extra room.

Our first stop was at the flour mill where my father had worked till the end, when the Germans picked him up. The mill which is at least seventy years old, still operates. It was owned before the war by three Jewish families. We were immediately surrounded and greeted by the workers who recognized that we were foreign visitors. The manager, a very friendly woman, allowed us to visit the mill and take pictures. We climbed all over inside the mill, looking for the place where my father hid me, my brother Julek, and my mother Genia during the roundups of Jews. This was, obviously, a very emotional moment for me.

I was not able to find out, reliably, what had happened to my father, since my mother, my brother, and I had left Horodenka earlier for the Ghetto in Tluste. We were shown at the Horodenka cemetery the graves of some of the last Jews who were brought there and shot by the Germans, so it is possible that this is also my father's last resting place.

The Jewish cemetery in Horodenka still exists, though many of the gravestones were removed by the Germans and their local assistants and used to pave the streets. It appears neglected and the overgrown vegetation is checked by grazing animals. The surrounding stone wall is gone, but we were told that the survivors in Israel are planning to have a fence erected. There are two mass graves: one for women and one for men, containing between 62 and 80 people. There is a beautiful memorial over one of the mass graves. It was erected recently by Edik, with the help of survivors in Israel, and has inscriptions in Hebrew and Ukrainian. The Hebrew plaque reads:

In memory of all the martyred victims of the Holocaust from Horodenka and vicinity who were murdered by the Nazis and their collaborators during the actions, in the labor camps, in the death camps, and by all other means during the period of the Second World War, 1941 - 1945.

The search for my home was futile: it had been bombed by the Germans and destroyed. The neighboring park had been extended all the way to the ruins of the Armenian church. This church and the former Catholic church (which is described by a plaque as an architectural landmark) now appear like medieval ruins. A single building remains of the Gymnasium (Polish high school). Most of the buildings in the former Jewish section around the Great Synagogue are gone, replaced by a large open air market. The Great Synagogue stands, its exterior appears to be in reasonably good condition. It is now used as a gymnasium and an ugly wing was attached to it. A plaque on the wall informs the visitor in Hebrew, Ukrainian, English, and Yiddish:

This is the site of the Great Synagogue of the Jewish Community that existed from 1742 till 1941. Half of this community of Horodenka and its vicinity were taken from here by the Nazis and murdered on Dec. 4, 1941. May the memory of the Holocaust Martyrs be blessed forever.

On the former Strzelecka Street, which had been part of the war-time ghetto, many old houses still stand. I found my grandmother's house, where my family had also lived during the war. One woman who now lives there closed her door, probably afraid that we had come to reclaim our home, but another woman was very friendly, invited us in and allowed us to take pictures of what had been my grandmother's kitchen and living room. I tried to find our hiding place in the attic, but the door was locked. I walked down the street, recognizing the homes of my uncle, my friends, and my neighbors. In Horodenka, the Germans achieved their objective: the town is quite "Judenfrei" – free of Jews. I had an eerie feeling walking on those familiar and yet so completely strange streets.

We then drove to Siemakowcze where, on December 4, 1941, 2,500 Jewish men, women, and children were murdered. There, on the mass grave, stands a simple monument, erected some time ago, with the dedication in Russian "To the Victims of Fascism". This was the only inscription which the communist regime would allow. After the demise of the USSR, a tablet was attached describing in Hebrew, Ukrainian, English, and Yiddish what happened on that fateful day:

Mass grave of 2,500 Jews – adults and children – from Horodenka and the vicinity who were murdered here by Nazis on Dec. 4, 1941. May the memory of the Holocaust victims be blessed forever.

Adjacent to the mass grave is a large camping complex, originally built by the communist trade unions for the vacationing of their members. In recent years, the Jewish Agency had rented this place as a summer camp for Jewish children from throughout Ukraine. I felt uneasy, picturing these Jewish children at play in this terrible place, but also gratified that there were Jewish children here, fifty years after Hitler's violent death. On this late summer day, the place was painfully quiet, the Dniester river flowed as majestically as it probably did on that sad winter day in 1941, and the lush landscape belied the unimaginable horror that happened there, in our generation...

Yes, there still is a town named Horodenka, but for me, the Horodenka of my childhood is to be found only in the far reaches of my memory.

Attachment 2

Speech at the Yom Hashoah Observance in Atlanta

April 18, 2004

INTRODUCTION

When I was asked if I would be willing to speak at today's commemoration of Yom Hashoah there was a good reason for my acceptence. The last words of my dying mother still ring in my ears: "someone must survive to tell the world", she repeated over and over again during that bitter winter of 1942. I feel duty bound to bear witness, yet words fail me to convey the horror. How could such slaughter occur in the heart of Europe?

We read in Ecclesiastes "ein chadash tachat ha'shemesh" there is nothing new under the sun. But Koheleth was wrong, such bestiality has never been seen under the sun. Six million innocents were murdered, 1 million children. Much has been written, much has been explored about this period in history, and much is yet to come, but Daniel Goldhagen wrote correctly that the armies of killers who descended on our towns and villages were, in his words, "Hitler's willing executioners".

MY SHTETL

My "shtetl" Horodenka, I am sure, was not unlike the towns and villages, some of you hail from. Jews lived there since the 17th century. Through the centuries different movements swept the region: there were adherents of Shabatai Zwi and followers of Baal Shem Tov, whose son-in-law, I believe, was buried in our cemetery. I remember our Hebrew class being brought to the little structure in the cemetery and asked to bring a "Pitka" a petition, a prayer to place there. No Petition, no prayer could avert the catastrophe that befell our people.

Zionists of every stripe earnestly debated the structure of a country that did not exist. Some made Aliya, others helped in any way they could. No household was without the little blue and white "pushka" of the Jewish National Fund, an ever present reminder of our hopes and longing to someday come to Eretz Israel.

There were of course those who taught that we must await the Messiah wherever we are. We waited and waited, but instead of redemption the killers came.

September 1st 1939 war broke out, a war which was to be so devastating to our people. A third of world Jewry will be murdered, great institution of learning, scholars, artists, poets will be lost.

When Poland was divided between Germany and the Soviet Union, our region was occupied by the Russians. Our people feared deportation to Siberia; little did they know then that exile to the frozen wastelands of Siberia was much preferable to what awaited us all.

When Germany attacked the Soviet Union, we watched with dismay as the much proclaimed undefeatable Soviet army crumbled initially.

Germans occupied our city in July and the reign of terror began. Ghetto, starvation, random killings. December 4, 1941, half of the Jewish population of our town 2,500 men women and children were murdered in a nearby forest of Siemakowce.

This systematic slaughter was repeated thousands of times, many times with full cooperation of the local population. The story of Jedwabne was not unique. Jan Gross tells in his book "Neighbors" how the Polish neighbors drove 800 Jews into a barn and set it afire. In numerous towns and villages our neighbors took the initiative even without the prodding of the Gestapo. In our area Ukrainian thugs drowned in the Dniester river hundreds of defenseless people...

"DEATH IS THE MASTER AUS DEUTSCHLAND" Paul Celan wrote in his heart wrenching poem "Death Fugue", but the master from Germany had many helpers.

Leaders of the free world knew quite well what was happening, but rescuing the Jews was not their priority. When Jan Karsky, the Polish underground courier gave a detailed account of what he had seen in the Warsaw ghetto and in the concentration camps, he was met with distrust. Even Justice Felix Frankfurter is quoted: "I am unable to believe what you told me".

MANY COULD NOT BELIEVE IT THEN, SOME ARE TRYING TO DENY IT NOW.

RESISTANCE

The survivors had to live with one of the most painful accusations made by ignorant people "they walked like sheep to slaughter". No one ever accused the over 500,000 Russian prisoners of war who were killed by the Germans of cowardice, or lack of resistance, yet the world expected heroic uprisings from defenseless civilian populations. And resist they did; surviving one more day in the ghetto was resistance, teaching Jewish children under the threat of death, as my mother did, was resistance; refusing to give up her Sabbath candlestick to the Germans, as my grandmother did, was resistance. In the dark of night we helped her bury them in the garden. I still dream that some day I might be able to dig them up and have them brighten my Sabbath table.

There was other resistance as well, in every ghetto, in every camp. Let us remember that the defenders of the Warsaw ghetto fought valiantly, knowing full well that victory or survival were impossible, they fought to die with honor. The starved and isolated members of the Jewish Defense Organization fought longer than the whole country of Poland with their standing army, air force and world support. They held out longer than the Maginot line in France.

There was resistance in the death camps, two crematoria were blown up in Auschwitz, there was resistance in Sobibor and Treblinka. Our partisans fought in lonely forests and far away fields. They were hounded not only by the SS and Ukrainian police, but they had to face the hostility of the local population. News reached us repeatetly in the labor camp of battles fought. Greatly outnumbered and outgunned, only few survived to tell the tale. Many lie in unmarked graves in distant forests and lonely fields.

Jews joined resistance fighters in every occupied country in Europe: France, Belgium, Italy, Yugoslavia, they fought in the Jewish Brigade of the British army.

LIBERATION

We all remember well the day we were liberated from concentration camps, labor camps, from hiding places, from far away forests. No matter were it occurred, the joy, if one can call it that, was mingled with great sorrow when we began to see and comprehend the enormity of the catastrophe that had befallen our people. All of us anxiously waited to go home, to search for any possible survivors, but for many of us the search was futile.

As we returned to our towns and villages, we found that strangers had occupied our homes. We were met with great hostility and threats to our lives. In the town of Kielce 60 Jews were murdered by Poles in 1946. When finally, in the year 2000, Prime Minister Wlodzimierz Cimoszewicz apologized to the Jewish people in the name of the Polish nation, he was severely reprimanded by father Henryk Jankowski who said "apologizing to the Jews is an insult to the Polish nation". One more proof that anti-Semitism can thrive even without Jews.

We gathered in abandoned houses, plastered many walls with notes searching for loved ones and friends, most of us wanted to leave that bloody continent forever. Some made it illegally to Palestine, some of us wound up in occupied Germany waiting to emigrate. Unlike our ancestors of long ago who fled from Egyptian slavery with gold and silver, some of us left Germany with what many Jewish professors, scientists, and scholars had contributed to that country: education. Tools which helped us to establish ourselves in our new homeland.

D. P. CAMPS

Some of you who wear the yellow ribbons today found yourselves once again in camps in the occupied zones of Germany. Not concentration camps, to be sure, but camps nevertheless. You did not invade the German towns and villages and plundered and robbed and exacted vengeance; instead, you built communal life, you established schools and synagogues and built families. Some of our second generation present here today were born in Displaced Persons Camps.

You bound your wounds and looked to the future. No armies of psychologists and social workers descended to help you deal with the severe traumas you had experienced, you did the best you could and tried to learn to live a normal life again.

When you finally reached these blessed shores, the kindest among your relatives or friends who met you, told you how lucky you were to have survived and urged you to forget the past and start a new life. To forget the past… as though that was possible or even permissible... You spent your days in struggles to adapt yourself to the new country, to learn a new language, to acquire professions, to start businesses. And many of you succeeded beyond your fondest dreams. Yet in your restless nights, in your dreams or nightmares your never left your "shtetl", you relived the horrors over and over again.

The holidays were the hardest for you. You filled the empty chairs that your parents, grandparents, uncles, aunts and cousins should have occupied, with friends, many friends. Perhaps, you thought, your children will not notice and ask why there were no relatives at their Seder table as there were among their American friends. And so, gently, you started to tell little by little about your family and the reason for their absence. Someone once asked a group of second generation young people when they first learned what happened to their families. The answer from all of them was – "I NEVER DID NOT KNOW". For some, it was the blue numbers on your arm, some of us had an invisible number branded with a searing iron on our hearts, the number 6 million.

SECOND GENERATION

You of the second generation, how was the memory of the Shoah transmitted to you? As Eva Hoffman writes "In the beginning was the war". And she continues, in the world she knew, people did not emerge from the womb but from war. The defining event you all have in common belongs to your prehistory, to the experiences of your parents. She refers to you as the "hinge generation" between the experience and memory of the Holocaust.

It is not an easy position in life, few of your contemporaries could understand you. And then came September 11, 2001, and more people began to comprehend what it was like to have your entire world shaken to its very foundations, as was the case with your parents' world.

Many of you are strongly committed to teach the world about the Shoah, and preserve and honor the memory of our martyred people. For that we are most grateful to you and thank you from the bottom of our hearts.

LESSONS LEARNED - LEGACY

A few months ago I was interviewed by an Emory student, a wonderful young woman, who wanted to know what are the lessons to be learned from the Shoah, what have we learned that we can pass on to future generations. The young earnestly seek to learn to understand, most importantly they wish for some redeeming quality to this great catastrophe. What can we tell them? That darkness covered the earth, that few cared and fewer did something about it. Yes, there were some brave and righteous people among the nations who risked their lives to help our people, to them we are forever grateful; but let us be frank, they were very, very few, hugely outnumbered by the killers and those who stood idly by and those who enriched themselves with the spoils.

Movies like "Schindler's List" and "The Pianist" are viewed widely and are accepted as history. It is soothing to think that there was also some light in that deep darkness. People around the world embraced the story of Anne Frank. I remember sitting in the theater in New York in silent shock as I heard the closing words of the play. "I still believe that people are good at heart". I wondered if Anne would have said the same words in Bergen Belsen as she watched helplessly her sister Margo dying of starvation and disease and felt her own life ebb away.

I know I would not have said those words the day I faced a firing squad, the day my 17 years old brother was killed. On that day, the world seemed to have been drained of all goodness.

What can we tell them? That justice was served? Few of the perpetrators ever stood before a court of law and answered for their crimes.

And yet, if history is not to be repeated, we must tell our stories, we must fight anti-Semitism in whatever disguise it appears and wherever we find it. We must struggle for victory over forgetfulness, saving the victims from a second death. We must fight against trivialization and exploitation of the Holocaust.

On this sacred ground we must pledge to bear witness, to remember and honor the memory of the millions of our people who perished in the Shoah.

The Location of Horodenka in Europe, 2007.

Places of Tosia's wartime experiences.

Tosia's mother Genia in a Purim costume.

Tosia's father Jacob (first row on the right)
with the Zaleszczyki amateur orchestra.

Mother and brother Julek.

Julek and Tosia.

Mother, Julek and Tosia.

Tosia after the end of the war.

Aboard the "Marine Flasher", on the way to the U.S.A.

Tosia and her sons (l. to r.) James, David, George.

On Tosia's and Fred's 50th wedding anniversary
(l. to r.): David, George, Tosia, Fred, James.

On Tosia's and Fred's 50th wedding anniversary (l. to r.): Zachary, Lilly, Tosia, Isabel, Fred, Benjamin, Samuel.

Tosia after retirement.